Called Unto His Eternal Glory

Called Unto His Eternal Glory

Lance Lambert

LANCE LAMBERT MINISTRIES

Richmond, Virginia, USA

ISBN: 978-1-68389-025-6
www.lancelambert.org

Contents

1.
Man is Destined for Glory

Matthew 17:1–8

And after six days Jesus taketh with him Peter, and James, and John his brother, and bringeth them up into a high mountain apart: and he was transfigured before them; and his face did shine as the sun, and his garments became white as the light. And behold, there appeared unto them Moses and Elijah talking with him. And Peter answered, and said unto Jesus, Lord, it is good for us to be here: if thou wilt, I will make here three tabernacles; one for thee, and one for Moses, and one for Elijah. While he was yet speaking, behold, a bright cloud overshadowed them: and behold, a voice out of the cloud, saying, This is my beloved Son, in whom I am well pleased; hear ye him. And when the disciples heard it, they fell on their face, and were sore afraid. And Jesus came and touched them and said, Arise, and be not afraid. And lifting up their eyes, they saw no one, save Jesus only.

1 Peter 5:10–11

And the God of all grace, who called you unto his eternal glory in Christ, after that ye have suffered a little while, shall himself perfect, establish, strengthen you. To him be the dominion for ever and ever. Amen.

1 Peter 4:12–13

Beloved, think it not strange concerning the fiery trial among you, which cometh upon you to prove you, as though a strange thing happened unto you: but insomuch as ye are partakers of Christ's sufferings, rejoice; that at the revelation of his glory also ye may rejoice with exceeding joy.

1 Peter 5:1

The elders therefore among you I exhort, who am a fellow-elder, and a witness of the sufferings of Christ, who am also a partaker of the glory that shall be revealed.

Shall we pray?

Beloved Lord, we are so thankful that we are found here in Your presence. We ask You, Lord, that You will surround this time with Your power and that You will touch everyone of our hearts and lives. We want very simply now to recognize that without You we can do nothing. We can speak many words, outline truths, give sound doctrine; but Lord, unless You are here and Your anointing is upon both the speaking and the hearing, then it will all be to no avail. But Lord, You are here, and You have provided an anointing for us that You have dearly won at Calvary and which the Holy Spirit makes a living reality and experience to each one of us. For the speaking of Your word and for the hearing of Your word we stand by faith into that anointing that we may know Your working in our hearts, touching us, changing us, that we may not be able to be the same again. Hear us, oh Lord, for we ask all this in the name of our Messiah, the Lord Jesus. Amen.

As I waited for the Lord to give me a word for this conference, finally, into my heart He breathed this word: "The God of all grace who has called you unto His eternal glory in Christ." In my estimation there is no substitute word for the word glory. Some modern versions have used the word splendor. Some have suggested the word magnificence. At other times they have thought to translate this word in both Hebrew and in Greek by the word honor. Actually, now and again it can be translated as honor, but none of these words convey the real meaning of glory. We have to leave it as glory, and the Holy Spirit has to reveal to us what glory is. It is the same with grace. Once you start to substitute the word unmerited favor, you have done damage, I think, to the word grace.

Grace has to be revealed to you. No amount of words can actually convey the word grace. Only God can reveal to the human heart what grace really means. It is the same with glory. The Spirit of God has to take this word, this concept, this truth, this reality, and He has to reveal it to us so that it becomes part of our own being.

What is Glory

What is glory? You remember in Exodus 40:34–35 that when the tabernacle was raised up and everything was in place it says:

"Then the cloud covered the tent of meeting, and the glory of the Lord filled the tabernacle. And Moses was not able to enter into the tent of meeting, because the cloud abode thereon, and the glory of the Lord filled the tabernacle."

After the temple of the Lord was built and completed and everything was in place and the ark of the Lord had been brought into it, then it says in II Chronicles 5:13–14: "It came to pass, when the trumpeters and singers were as one, to make one sound to be heard in praising and thanking the Lord; and when they lifted up their voice with the trumpets and cymbals and instruments of music, and praised the Lord, saying, For he is good; for his steadfast love endureth for ever; that then the house was filled with a cloud, even the house of the Lord, so that the priests could not stand to minister by reason of the cloud: for the glory of the Lord filled the house of God."

What is glory? We often think of glory as the President pinning medals on chests, a certain sort of reward for battles won or for bravery or something else, whether in the army or in civilian life. But glory is not medals being pinned on the chest, brass bands playing, and wonderful, rousing kinds of anthems being sung.

What is glory? The Lord can sometimes speak to us but He does not manifest His presence. He can actually work without manifesting His presence. But when He manifests His presence, that is glory. So here you have the most extraordinary thing. The presence of the Lord had been with the people and spoken with Moses. He had done so many acts before them in delivering them from Egypt and keeping them, but suddenly the presence of the Lord was manifested and the tabernacle was filled with the glory of the Lord. No one could stand; no one could enter. It was the same with the temple. God did so many things through King David in all the preparations for the temple and all the wonderful defeats of the enemies of God, but when the temple was finally complete and the ark was brought in, then the presence of the Lord was manifested. As I see it, it is the presence of the Lord manifested.

The God of Glory Appeared to Abraham

We have a wonderful word in Acts 7:2: "When our father Abraham was in Ur of the Chaldees in Mesopotamia, the God of glory appeared to him." Is that just a title for the Lord? What does it mean "the God of glory appeared to Abraham"?

Ur was one of the great aristocratic, Babylonian, Babel complex of cities and it was the city Abraham actually lived in. According to our tradition, his family was in charge of idol making—no small business. Every single corner of every street had an idol. Every home had a household god and a kitchen god. There were idols everywhere. Here, there, and everywhere were idols. It was a very lucrative business to be in. Everyone needed idols. The wheel of life could not go round without idols. The temples were filled with idols.

Then the God of glory appeared to Abraham. When God manifested His presence, something happened to Abraham that was to change history. He was never the same again. For him, Ur of the Chaldees, money-making, and all the rest of it faded into insignificance. It was the glory of the Lord, the God of glory, that appeared to him. He went out not knowing where he was going except that the Lord had told him to go. You know the rest of the story. It was the manifested presence of God.

Moses Saw God's Glory

I think also of Moses. The Lord actually spoke with Moses. In one place He spoke so gloriously that Moses had to put a veil on his face because the people could not even look at him. It was so dazzling, so brilliant. He had seen miracle after miracle. He had seen the ten plagues come on Egypt. He had seen miracles done in the presence of the leader of the greatest superpower of the world at that time. And he had seen the Lord bring out the slaves, the children of Israel from Egypt. They had seen the Red Sea split in two, and they had gone over as on dry ground. Then when Pharaoh's crack forces followed swiftly, the sea closed in on them and drowned them all. They had seen a pillar of cloud by day and a pillar of fire by night all through their journey. They had seen the manna six days out of seven and a double portion on the sixth to cover the seventh. They had seen the acts of the Lord. But the extraordinary thing is that this knowledge of the Lord, this being a recipient of messages from God Himself inflamed Moses with a hunger for more.

So in Exodus 33 he said, (I quote the modern version): "Please show me Your glory." Most children of God, most Christians would surely say, "Moses had already seen the glory of God. He had seen the mountain smoke with fire. He had seen and heard the voice of God like a trumpet reverberating and shaking the very ground so that the people of Israel were on their faces in fear. He had seen the finger of God write the ten words on tablets of stone." But Moses knew there was something more. So he said, "Show me Your glory." And the Lord said, "You cannot see My face and live; you shall stand by Me. (In Hebrew it says 'with Me.') You shall stand on the rock, and as My glory passes by, I will put you in the cleft of the rock and cover you with My hand." What was it? It was the manifested presence of God.

The Glory of the Lord Jesus

I think of our Lord Jesus. "The Word became flesh, and dwelt among us (and we beheld His glory, glory as of the only begotten of the Father), full of grace and truth." Jesus was the manifested presence of God. He manifested it in the very first miracle He did when He turned water into wine at the marriage feast of Cana. Many Christians would have wished He had turned wine into water, but He turned water into wine, real wine not grape juice. It was the best wine. It is incredible. You would have hardly said that was manifesting His glory but it was, because it was a wedding and Jesus was saying, "I have come for a bride." The corruptible water of human life can become the incorruptible wine of the Spirit of God. Once the Lord gets into a person He turns water into wine, not wine into water. Now there are alcoholics where the Lord needs to turn wine into water. But generally speaking, God turns the corruptible water of our human nature and life into the incorruptible wine of the Spirit of life in Christ Jesus. It is manifested glory. "We beheld His glory, glory as of the only begotten of the Father full of grace and truth."

The Glory in the City

In Revelation 21:23: "And the city hath no need of the sun, neither of the moon, to shine upon it: for the glory of God did lighten it, and the lamp thereof is the Lamb."

"The glory of God did lighten it." This is a most interesting thing. We sing hymns about treading the streets of gold and going through the pearly gates. I have no doubt at all that there will be an actual capital city in the coming kingdom of God. I do not belong to the kind of theology that believes we are all going to float away into space and live forever there, somehow suspended in space playing harps. I do not find this idea of heaven in my Bible. It is so prevalent among Christians, but I cannot find such a thing. I have looked everywhere to find it. People say, "We are going to heaven." I do not understand what they are talking about. From my understanding of the word of God, Jesus brings us back to this earth, and if you do believe in the Millennium it does not disappear. There will be a new heaven and a new earth wherein dwells righteousness. You and I were not made to live in space. We were created human beings. God has a special design in us.

I have no doubt this city that we read about will have a located headquarters where the King and His government are for all eternity. But this city is a bride and therefore it is a spiritual reality first and foremost. The gates are symbolic; they have significance. There is only one street in this enormous city. The whole thing is gold, transparent as crystal. You have never seen gold like it. Who would wear gold if it were transparent? It just does not seem to be gold anymore.

This city is like an electric light bulb. The thing about this city is light and the light is the glory of God, the manifested presence of God, shining out from that city into the darkness. The nations, it says, will walk in the light of it. There is no need of the sun or the moon because the glory of God is the light.

The Glory to be Revealed to Mankind

Is this matter of glory relevant to us? I believe it is very relevant because we are called unto His eternal glory in Christ. It is not transient glory, not a glorious flash of light but eternal, permanent, forever, limitless, without end. We are called unto His eternal glory in Christ unworthy as we are. It is the God of all grace who calls you and me.

I do not know how you view yourself. Some people have a very high estimate of themselves and when they fall, or make a mistake, or fail, or even sin, they cannot get over it. They have this idea that God is so shocked that He is always holding His head and saying, "I would not have saved them if I had known that they could do this kind of thing." But God knows the worst about you. He knows your capacity for depravity; only some of us have a cultural background that keeps us from it. He knows your ability to sin, your ability to be lost in evil. He knows it all and He saved you. He is the God of all grace. Unworthy as you and I are, unprofitable as we are, yet He redeemed us. All of us were nothing but a load of trouble to the Lord. He could well do without us. (If I had been the Lord I would have stopped the whole thing right at the beginning. I would not have bothered with anyone. I would have said if that is how they feel, if that is the choice they make, let them go. We will annihilate them all and we will start again with a new race. You can be thankful I am not the Lord.) The Lord is very different—full of grace.

The God of all grace has called the unworthy debris of mankind to His eternal glory in Christ. I do not know if you realize just how wonderful it is, but it is wonderful. This is why the apostle Paul says this in Ephesians 4 about this calling: "I therefore the prisoner in the Lord beseech you to walk worthily of the calling wherewith you were called."

In II Corinthians 4:4,6: "In whom the god of this world hath blinded the minds of the unbelieving, that the light of the gospel of the glory of Christ, who is the image of God, should not dawn upon them. Seeing it is God, that said, Light shall shine out of darkness, who shined in our hearts, to give the light of the knowledge of the glory of God in the face of Jesus Christ."

If you have been saved it was not your doing. For the god of this world has blinded the minds of all who are unsaved lest they should see the light of the gospel of the glory of Christ. But it is God who said, "Let there be light, and there was light." And over you He said, "Let there be light." And somehow into your heart light shone. You may not put it in these words, but this is the truth in reality. It was the light of the knowledge of the glory of God in the face of Jesus the Messiah. There is no other way to be saved. This is the calling that you and I have.

In Romans 9:23 it says, "And that God might make known the riches of his glory upon vessels of mercy, which he afore prepared unto glory, even us, whom he also called, not from the Jews only, but also from the Gentiles." Vessels of mercy. Are you a vessel of mercy? Long before you were a twinkle in your parents' eyes, long before you were ever thought of by grandparents or great-grandparents, God made preparation for you. He prepared you as a vessel of mercy for glory. Man was originally created and designed for the glory of God; not to the glory of God only, but for glory, the glory of God.

Man Fell Short of the Glory of God

"For all have sinned (there is no difference) and fall short of the glory of God" (Romans 3:23). If I were coming from New York to Los Angeles by air and the fare was $300.00 and I had $290.00, I could not get the ticket. It makes no difference whether you have $290.00 or $50.00, you have fallen short of the price.

Some people are naturally sweeter, nobler, and more decent, but we have all fallen short. All of us. What have we fallen short of? Oh, you say, eternal life. It does not say so. (Of course, it is to do with eternal life.) What have we fallen short of? The kingdom of heaven. It does not say so. It is true. What have we fallen short of? We have fallen short of the glory of God—that for which we were created and designed; we have fallen short of it through sin.

There is no point to human life without glory. I will say it again. There is no point to human life, to your being born, without glory. You were designed and created for glory. Without glory you are an animal. You are just an animal. You have a transient, temporal life that has no meaning. You live for time, you live for the things of sense, you live for money, or sex, or career, or something else. But in a moment of time you will be snuffed out. Corruption and death make your life pointless! You can go to Christian meetings, but unless the Spirit of God is doing a work in you, your life is pointless. There is no point to it. You might as well be an animal. Now there may be some animal lovers here who will be very upset with me. I love animals and I would like to think that all the ones I have had passed on to their reward, but I cannot find it anywhere in the Book. All I can believe is that sometime God may recreate such animals. I do not know; that is a little bit of speculation.

But what is not speculation is this: you were created as a human being and designed as a human being for glory. And if you fall short of glory, your life is pointless, it is rubbish. When Jesus calls hell ghenna, in Hebrew hinnom, which is the valley I live in in Jerusalem, what He is saying is this: It is the rubbish dump, the trash dump. If you fall short of the glory of God your life is rubbish. It is pointless. It has no meaning or significance. You have totally missed the point.

Glorified man, not sinful man, lies at the heart of God's universe. Did you know that? In Romans 8:18-21 it says, "For I reckon that the sufferings of this present time are not worthy to be compared with the glory which shall be revealed to us-ward. For the earnest expectation of the creation [natural creation] waiteth for the revealing of the sons of God. For the creation was subjected to vanity [futility], not of its own will, but by reason of him who subjected it, in hope that the creation itself also shall be delivered from the bondage of corruption into the liberty of the glory of the children of God."

That means that this universe, this earth, this world in which we are found and are making such a mess of is all waiting. If we had a special kind of hearing apparatus, we could hear a bush, or a tree, or a plant; we could hear an animal, or a bird, or the fish of the sea. If we could hear it, they are all groaning with a travail because they were not responsible for being subjected to futility. But when man fell and fell short of the glory of God, when he sinned, then the whole earth as we know it, the firmament was subjected to futility. And if we had that ear to hear, it is all groaning, waiting for the glory of the children of God.

One of our prophets said thousands of years ago: "The earth shall be covered with the knowledge of the glory of God as the waters cover the sea" (see Isaiah 11:9).

Does that give a new dimension of understanding to you on the question of the God of all grace? Can you believe that this God, this living God, this God of ours is so full of grace that He has called you and me to His eternal glory in Christ? If you know your unworthiness, it is enough to make you weep. If you knew how unprofitable you are, you would weep. But God loves us so much. He always has the end product in view. Are we not a difficult people? I have lived long enough among the people of God to know we are difficult people. Oh, we sometimes like to think how sweet we all are. I do not think there is such a lot of sweetness, not when it is put to pressure. It vanishes very rapidly. It is amazing to me that the God of all grace has called you and me to His eternal glory in Christ Jesus.

Glory is in Christ

Here is another point I want to make. It is "in Christ." The God of all grace has called us unto His eternal glory in Christ. There is no glory of God apart from Christ. Oh, the amazing grace and love of God calling us to share in Christ's glory. Can you believe it? The Lord Jesus has a glory which is unique to Him. After all, He has always existed. He is God the Son. And there is a glory which is unique to Him and which you and I can never share. But there is also a glory in Christ that you and I are called to share.

Hebrews 1:3 says, "God has spoken to us in His Son, whom He appointed heir of all things, through whom also He made the worlds; who being the effulgence of His glory, and the very image of His substance, and upholding all things by the word of His power, when He had made purification of sins, sat down on the right hand of the Majesty on high."

This "effulgence of glory" is a terrible word, isn't it? Some of the modern versions say "outshining" or "shining." Actually, it is even more than that. It means the "radiant outshining" of glory. Jesus is the radiant outshining of glory.

In the original, "The exact impress of the substance of God" or "the image of God," means that when I see Jesus by the Spirit of God, I see God. I understand the heart of God. I understand the mind of God. The more I get to know the Lord Jesus, the more I get to know God.

Again, in John 1:14: "The Word became flesh, and dwelt among us (and we beheld his glory, glory as of the only begotten from the Father)." He dwelt among us and He manifested a kind of glory that He wants us in the end to share. It is something so amazing.

In John 17:4 Jesus is praying: "I glorified Thee on the earth, having accomplished the work which Thou hast given Me to do. And now, Father, glorify Thou Me with Thine own self with the glory which I had with Thee before the world was." What an amazing word!

"And the glory which Thou hast given Me I have given unto them; that they may be one, even as We are one; I in them, and Thou in Me, that they may be perfected into one; that the world may know that Thou didst send Me, and lovedst them, even as Thou lovedst me. Father, I desire that they also whom Thou hast given Me be with Me where I am, that they may behold My glory" (John 17:22).

Are you one of those given by the Father to the Son? Have you been given by the Father to the Son? Then this prayer of the Lord Jesus will certainly be answered—that you may share His glory, that you may become a recipient of His glory, that you may become an outshining of His glory. In other words, you will reach the end for which you were created and designed. We hardly know what it will mean, what we will do, but it is wonderful just to think about it.

Romans 8:15: "For ye received not the spirit of bondage again unto fear; but ye received the spirit of adoption [placing], whereby we cry, Abba, Father. The Spirit himself beareth witness with our spirit, that we are children of God: and if children, then heirs; heirs of God, and joint-heirs with Christ; if so be that we suffer with him, that we may be also glorified with him."

"Heirs of God, joint-heirs with Christ." Oh, what a calling you have dear child of God! Why do you look all the time at the mud, the muck, the filth, the weakness, the mistakes, the sins? Look up. You have an incredible calling. You are called to be heirs of God and joint-heirs with Christ. The Spirit of God has been shed abroad in your heart with the most intimate word in His mouth, Abba, Father. What an unbelievable thing this is—this glory in Christ!

The Transfiguration

How do you understand the transfiguration of the Lord Jesus? I think most Christians have no idea about it. It is one of the great stages in Christ's ministry and life, along with His birth, His baptism, and so on. Most Christians look upon what happened on the mount (some people say it is Mount Tabor but I personally think it is Mount Hermon) as a spotlight suddenly shining out from heaven on the Lord Jesus and lighting Him up. Nonsense! It was not a divine spotlight from heaven that circled around the Lord Jesus so that He appeared to be unique, special. Something happened in the Lord Jesus. Something was switched on inside of Him, and suddenly His hair, His skin, His clothes radiated light. That is transfiguration.

There is not a child of God in this place who will not be transfigured. When the Lord comes and we are alive, in the twinkling of an eye, so fast, this mortal shall put on immortality and this corruptible shall put on incorruption, and we shall be like Him in a moment!

This means that the life of God in us, the Spirit of God who has come within us, the indwelling of the Lord Jesus Himself, in a moment of time God will flick a switch and the glory will be manifested.

Jesus, as Man, Reached the Glory of God

From the beginning you were meant to have glory. When God created Adam and Eve, although He knew it would not happen, His whole idea was that they should take of the tree of life in the midst of the garden and then be transfigured. There would be a time of training and discipline but they would have been transfigured in glory. But they sinned and fell short of the glory of God. Then the Lord Jesus stepped onto the stage, not as God but as man. He is the second Man, the last Adam, and He stepped onto the stage. He was tempted in all points like as we are, yet without sin. And He reached the glory. Where Adam fell short, Jesus succeeded. Where Adam fell short and fell, Jesus reached the glory of God as a man.

At that point Jesus, as a man, could have stepped into heaven. (I do not know how else to put it.) But He did not. Having reached the glory of God, He turned around and came down and symbolically He met an epileptic lad full of demons. He was one week from Calvary. Having reached the glory of God as a man, He set His face as a flint to Calvary. Why? Because He wanted to bring many sons unto glory (see Hebrews 2:10). He wanted you and me to share His glory. He knew there was no chance unless He went to the cross. Is it any wonder that in I Corinthians 2:8 the Lord Jesus is called the Lord of glory?

If you and I have been called to God's eternal glory, if it is the God of all grace who has called us, if this glory of God is in Christ and in Christ alone, there is an unfailing determination on the part of the Lord Jesus to see that we get there. The more I go on with the Lord, the farther I feel I am away from the glory of God. It is a comfort to me that early on in the ministry of the apostle Paul he calls himself the least of all saints, but at the very end he calls himself the chief of all sinners. The further he went on with the Lord the more conscious he was of how hopeless he was. In the end he spoke those words of faith: "I fought the fight, I finished the course, and there is laid up for me a crown of righteousness."

So it has to be with every one of us. I am a Calvinist. I believe that long before I was saved God had prepared for me. I do not believe in a god who accommodates Himself to human circumstances. Then he is an idol. He can only think what you think, He can only say what you say, He can only do what you allow Him to do. I believe in a God who is infinite. And I think the most wonderful thing for me is His unfailing determination to bring me to glory.

I think of the Scripture in Jude 24, "Now unto him that is able to guard you from stumbling, and to set you before the presence of his glory without blemish in exceeding joy, to the only God our Saviour, through Jesus Christ our Lord, be glory, majesty, dominion and power, before all time, and now, and for evermore. Amen."

Writing to the Philippian church, the apostle said, "Being confident of this very thing, that He who began a good work in you will perform it until the day of Jesus Christ" (Philippians 1:6).

Don't you think that is wonderful? Don't you think this is also wonderful in II Corinthians 2:14: "But thanks be unto God, who always leadeth us in triumph in Christ, and maketh manifest through us the savor of his knowledge in every place."

God's Requirement

There is only one thing God requires of you, only one thing. It is utter simplicity. It is obedience. When you and I have an argument with the Lord, when we murmur, when we rebel, then we nullify the grace of God. Isn't that a terrible thought? We can neutralize this unfailing determination of the God of all grace to bring us to glory. We can nullify His endeavor by disobedience.

Is there anybody here who has not disobeyed the Lord at some point? We have all done it. When it is confessed and put right, we learn from our mistakes, our sins, our transgressions, our disobedience. But I have lived long enough to see children of God who have lived in disobedience all their lives. They have become nothing but memorials, grave stones. They are like a graveyard: Here lies the body of so and so, born so and so, died so and so. Once they were alive spiritually. Once they walked with the Lord. Once they breathed in the breath of God. Now they are monuments.

Child of God, it is not worth it. It is not worth it. If you were to gain the whole world and build the biggest business empire, if you were to reach the top of your profession, if you were to somehow make so much money that you could buy a dozen palaces, it is not worth it if in so doing you have cut yourself out of the race. It is not worthwhile because you were designed for God's glory, created for His glory, and only when you get there will you understand just how much you were created for it and just how much you were designed for it. It is all worthwhile—all the sufferings, all the difficulties, all the problems if God can do something. "After that you have suffered a little while, shall Himself perfect, establish, strengthen you." May the Lord do it for every one of us.

Shall we pray?

Beloved Lord, You have called us to Your eternal glory in Christ. Let this truth dawn on us this night. By Your Spirit make it a living reality to every one of us and if we are living lives in disobedience, Lord, haunt us this night. Give us no rest, no peace. Haunt us, Lord, until in the end we confess our disobedience and find our way back to You. Lord, there is nothing more wonderful than Your unfailing determination to bring us to glory. Help us, oh Lord, for we ask it in the name of our Messiah, the Lord Jesus. Amen.

2.
Christ in You: the Certain Hope of Glory

1 Peter 5:10–11

And the God of all grace, who called you unto his eternal glory in Christ, after that ye have suffered a little while, shall himself perfect, establish, strengthen you. To him be the dominion for ever and ever. Amen.

Colossians 1:24–29

Now I rejoice in my sufferings for your sake, and fill up on my part that which is lacking of the afflictions of Christ in my flesh for his body's sake, which is the church; whereof I was made a minister, according to the dispensation of God which was given me to you-ward, to fulfil the word of God, even the mystery which hath been hid for ages and generations: but now hath it been manifested to his saints, to whom God was pleased to make known what is the riches of the glory of this mystery among the Gentiles, which is Christ in you, the hope of glory: whom we proclaim, admonishing every man and teaching every man in all wisdom, that we may present every man [full grown] perfect in Christ; whereunto I labor also, striving according to his working, which worketh in me mightily.

Colossians 2:6–7

As therefore ye received Christ Jesus the Lord, so walk in him, rooted and builded up in him, and established in your faith, even as ye were taught, abounding in thanksgiving.

Colossians 3:1–4

If then ye were raised together with Christ, seek the things that are above, where Christ is, seated on the right hand of God. Set your mind on the things that are above, not on the things that are upon the earth. For ye died, and your life is hid with Christ in God. When Christ, who is our life, shall be manifested,

then shall ye also with him be manifested in glory.

Ephesians 3:14–21

For this cause I bow my knees unto the Father, from whom every [the whole] family in heaven and on earth is named, that he would grant you, according to the riches of his glory, that ye may be strengthened with power through his Spirit in the inward man; that Christ may dwell in your hearts through faith; to the end that ye, being rooted and grounded in love, may be strong to apprehend with all the saints what is the breadth and length and height and depth, and to know the love of Christ which passeth knowledge, that ye may be filled unto all the fulness of God.

Now unto him that is able to do exceeding abundantly

Shall we pray?

Beloved Lord, we are so thankful that we can come like this into Your presence. We are not asking You to join us; we are joining You. We are coming into Your presence. You are the one who has called us together. And Lord, we want to thank You that You have provided an anointing for our time together. We want to stand by faith into that anointing, both for the speaking of Your word and the hearing of Your word. Dear Lord, let this be a time when we meet with Yourself, when something of Your word comes to dwell in us. Oh Lord, hear our cry and meet with us, for we ask it in the name of our Lord Jesus, the Messiah. Amen.

I have had on my heart that phrase in the first letter of the apostle Peter: "And the God of all grace who called you unto His eternal glory in Christ" (1 Peter 5:10). There is no substitute word for the word glory. Some modern versions have tried to use different words like honor, like magnificence, like splendor, but none of these words are adequate. Really there is no alternative word. We have to use the word glory, just as we have to use the word grace. Grace is grace. But the Holy Spirit has to reveal the meaning of glory just as He has to reveal the meaning of grace. It is the birthright of every child of God to know this mystery, the riches of His glory among the Gentiles. Only the Lord can reveal this to us. Grace and glory are twins. You cannot have glory without grace. They are twins; they belong together. The only way a human being will ever reach the glory of God is by the grace of God.

There is a beautiful phrase in a greatly loved Psalm that I think many people read and perhaps it does not sink in. It is Psalm 84. "How lovely are your tabernacles...The Lord will give grace and glory." The way to glory is through the grace of God.

Now I want to consider Colossians 1:27: "To whom God was pleased to make known what is the riches of the glory of this mystery among the Gentiles, which is Christ in you, the hope of glory."

It is not Christ for you. That is wonderful, but it is not Christ for you, the hope of glory. Although you cannot have any hope of glory if Christ is not for you.

It is not Christ above you. You cannot come to the glory of God if the Lord Jesus is not your Lord. He has to be your Lord.

It is not Christ before you. Of course, if you do not keep your eye on the Lord Jesus, you will never come to the glory of God. But it does not say that.

It is not Christ behind you. I fear this is what most Christians have. They have Christ behind them. He is always there, as it were, to clean up the messes, always there to overcome the mistakes, always there to get us back on the road. Every child of God knows Christ behind them. They try to live the Christian life and of course they make a mess of it. We all do; we are born that way. No human being can live the Christian life. Every one of us has to learn by experience, generally by failing and falling. We want the Lord to be behind us: "Help me, Lord. Help me, Lord. Get behind me, Lord. Support me, Lord. Be, as it were, the one who is coming up behind me, cleaning up the mess I am making." It is not Christ for you nor Christ above you nor Christ behind you; it is Christ in you.

There are not so many Christians who have ever had that revelation. Yet it is an essential part of the birthright of every child of God. It has to be revealed. What a difference it makes when suddenly you realize He is in you. He is in you.

The Son is Revealed in Us

It says in Galatians 1:15: "But when it was the good pleasure of God, who separated me, even from my mother's womb, and called me through his grace, to reveal his Son in me."

The apostle Paul's ministry began when the Spirit of God revealed Jesus in him. You remember that on the Damascus road he saw the Lord. The Lord actually spoke to him. The Lord revealed Himself to him. Then at some point, maybe in the three years in Arabia which this letter goes on to talk about, or maybe it was when Ananias laid his hand upon him, that suddenly he understood he was born of God, he was a child of God. To that Jesus who said, "I am Jesus whom you persecute," the apostle Paul would naturally have said: "I am not persecuting You; You are dead. You have gone. I cannot get at You. I am getting at all of these people who are causing all the problems among us, these disciples of Yours. They are the problem."

But it suddenly came home to the apostle Paul that when he touched those disciples, he touched the Lord Jesus. In touching them, he was touching the Lord Jesus. Is that where suddenly he understood that when he was born of God, when he was saved by the grace of God the Holy Spirit said, "Now you are part of the Lord Jesus. Now anyone who touches you, Paul, touches Me, His Son." "When it pleased God to reveal His Son in me."

I remember when I was first saved. I only knew the Lord objectively. Now I must say that there is a danger in thinking of the Lord Jesus as bread, thinking of the Lord Jesus as water, thinking of the Lord Jesus as the air we breathe, thinking of the Lord Jesus as life, thinking of the Lord Jesus as power. There is a danger. We become so subjective that we forget that there is a Man at the right hand of God. We forget that this Jesus is at the right hand of God. He is waiting to return. He still has marks in His hands. He still has a scar in His side. He still has the marks in His feet. He has not aged one whit in the thousands of years since He ascended to the right hand of God. And this Jesus is returning as King. He is coming back of all places (it might be a shock to some) to Jerusalem. There He will be crowned—this Jesus.

But How?

When I was first saved I only knew the Lord Jesus objectively. I remember the day I saw Him. I do not know how it was, in dream or vision, but I saw Him. And I remember the words to this day that He spoke to me. I was only fourteen years of age.

I tried to be such a good Christian. I read all about John Wesley and how he spoke to one person a day about their soul's salvation. So I determined I would do the same. I filled my mouth with Canaanite phraseology—the language of the Christians around me. They were Baptists, good people, born of God. I filled my mouth with their language. I spoke like they did. I had reasonable intelligence, and it did not take me long to learn the lingo. I did everything to make myself a good Christian. I think my zeal knew no end.

When I went to university, I was the terror of the students because I spoke to at least one a day about their salvation. It went something like this: "You are a sinner and I am a Christian. You are unsaved; I am saved. I am going to heaven; you are going to hell." More or less, that is the way I believed I had to do it. The result was that every time I walked along one of those corridors or hallways every student vanished into doors on either side. I have oftened wondered how many got into lectures that were nothing to do with their studies. Here was someone studying Japanese who got into the class on or Swahili or something else. I always remember how they vanished. I always had a place in the student common room because whenever I went in they melted away, and I was able to find a place to sit.

But I was desperate inside my own heart because although I knew what a Christian should be, somehow there was a discrepancy between what I was and what the Bible said I should be. My old pastor, Alan Redpath, who spotted that I was in trouble, sent in the post a little booklet But How? When I got this little blue booklet, I thought to myself: But How? I had said that again and again and again. Every time the pastor preached about victory in Christ, and we are more than conquerors, I thought, but how? Every time they sang the wonderful hymns about my chains falling off, I thought: but how? Or when we sang another hymn about the guilt and power of sin, I thought: but how? It was always with me: But how? But how? We heard wonderful things but all the time, the one question in my heart was: But how?

I took this little booklet and went to one of the dustiest, smelliest, old parish churches, right next to the School of Oriental and African Studies, and I got on my knees. The place was clausdephobic from the smell of dust. I doubt if anyone had cleaned the windows in a hundred years, and the smell from the cushions in the pews was just dust of a hundred years. But it was heaven opened for me. As I read that little booklet it was as if heaven itself opened, and I remember very clearly the first thing that came to me as an enormous shock was: the Holy Spirit is yours. I thought to myself: I hardly know there is a Holy Spirit. I know the Father. I know the Son, but the Holy Spirit—who is He? It came as a revelation to me that the only way that I could know Jesus, know what it was to have His life and power was through the Holy Spirit. And the Spirit of God whispered in my heart: "I have been given to you with all the keys to your life but you have stolen them." It was then that I said to the Lord: "Oh, forgive me. I have completely ignored You, dear Holy Spirit. I have hidden the keys. They are Yours. You have the keys to every part of my life."

The second thing that came home to me as revelation was that the Holy Spirit has been given to me to reproduce the life and nature of the Lord Jesus in me. That was a tremendous revelation for me. It was a revelation that Christ was in me by the Holy Spirit.

I was getting up from my knees when a third thing came to me: "My estimate of you is that I crucified you." That was a revelation to me. I had been trying to make old Lance Lambert a good Christian. I studied the word; I prayed; I had zeal; I was witnessing to everybody. Oh, what a revelation it was that God had crucified me. What had I been doing trying to make that old Lance a Christian when God had crucified him?

I got up from my knees and the Lord said, "Just wait, there is one more thing." I got down on my knees and the Lord said to me something that I do not think He would necessarily say to you: "No more witnessing. Unless I give you the opportunity, no more witnessing."

"Oh, Lord," I said, "okay."

Now for the first time He was Lord, and for three weeks I had a ball. I never witnessed to a soul and enjoyed the Lord. I so enjoyed the Lord. I thought I had been saved. I thought: "I have never been saved. I thought I was saved, but I wasn't saved. Now I am saved." Oh, it was so wonderful, just to be a human being and not to bother about myself anymore.

After three weeks one of the fellows on the rugby team for the college came up to me in the common room and said, "Can I ask you a very personal question?"

"Yes," I said, "please do."

He said, "We fellows have been talking. There is something different about you and us."

Now if had asked me that four weeks before I would have said, "Oh yes, you are a sinner and I am saved. You are going to hell and I am going to heaven." Then I would have asked him to come with me to a meeting. But this time I stared at him and I felt almost embarrassed. I said, "Well, we are both sinners, but I think the difference is that by the grace of God He has saved me." Then to my utter amazement tears ran down his cheeks.

Then I thought to myself: "There is something funny here. I have been trying to get someone saved for two whole years and

I have not succeeded once. Now suddenly a person walks up that I have not witnessed to and he says with tears coming down his cheeks in a crowded student room, 'How can I know God like you?'"

I said to him: "You have to ask the Lord Jesus into your heart. Confess that you are a sinner. Ask the Lord Jesus."

"Where can I do that?" he said. "In a church?"

"No," I said, "you can do it anywhere."

Then he said, "Can I do it here?"

I was so amazed my mouth dropped open and I said, "Well, yes, of course."

Then he lifted up his head and said, "Oh, God, You know what a sinner I am. Come into my heart, Lord Jesus, and save me."

That was the beginning of my ministry. God revealed the Lord Jesus in me. Now this is not for special people; this is for every child of God. Your family situation could be transformed. "Oh," you say, "I have a terrible husband. I have a terrible wife. I have terrible children. I have terrible parents." No, I am not talking about them; I am talking about you. God could so change you that in the end there is an impact in your family, your business, whatever problems you have. This is your birthright, to know that Christ, by the Holy Spirit, is in you. He is not only for you but also in you. This is so tremendous once you begin to understand it because everything is there for you.

You remember how the Lord Jesus put it in John 15:4: "Abide in me and I in you." If you are a child of God, the glorious fact is that your position is in Christ, and if you are in Christ by God's grace, Christ is in you. Maybe you do not know it. Maybe it has never come home to you with revelation.

The Only Hope of Glory

Let me take you a step further. Christ in you is the only hope you have of glory. There is no other hope. In you He is the hope of glory. I am a Jew; you are a Gentile. The riches of the glory of this mystery is among the Gentiles. Isn't that amazing! Yet, most of you who have got Gentile background do not even know that Christ is in you. There are so many trying to be Christians, trying to be good Christians, trying to be zealous Christians. You will wear yourself out. You will exhaust yourself so much in trying to be a Christian that there will be no joy in it; only misery. That is not the Christian life. The gospel is joy and peace and righteousness in the Holy Spirit. The only way the Christian life can be the genuine article is when God touches the eyes of your heart and you see He is living in you. I hope I have made it clear enough: Christ in you—glory. One day the manifested presence of God will be in your redeemed body.

In Colossians 2:9-10 it says, "For in him dwelleth all the fulness of the Godhead bodily, and in him ye are made full [complete]."

God has placed everything in the Lord Jesus. Outside of the Lord Jesus there is nothing. There is a divine veto on everything outside of the Lord Jesus. That is religion, Christian religion, or any kind of religion. It is just religion. But in Christ God has given us everything—all the blessings, all the fulness, all the provision, all the life, and all the power. Everything you need is in the Lord Jesus. "In him dwelleth all the fulness of the Godhead bodily, and in him you are made full or complete."

Rich in Christ

In Ephesians 1:3 it says, "Blessed be the God and Father of our Lord Jesus Christ, who hath blessed us with every spiritual blessing in the heavenly places in Christ."

Where are these blessings, every spiritual blessing? In Christ—every one of them. Thank God, we do not experience all of them at once. We would be in a mental home. There is no way you and I could experience all the blessings of God. Can you imagine it! We could not contain them. We would go mad. It would unhinge us mentally. But by the grace of God it is little by little, step by step, stage by stage. There is a blessing for everything. Every blessing is yours in Christ. Every promise is yours in Christ.

There are thousands of promises. In II Corinthians 1:20 it says, "In Him is the Yes and through Him is the Amen." God has, as it were, said, "In My Son I say 'Yes' to every promise in the Book." Of course, the Holy Spirit has to apply it. When we come into situations, when we are facing problems, when we have circumstances that do not seem to be very happy, then the Holy Spirit takes one of these promises and it becomes ours. We stand on it and through Him is the fulfillment. In Him, yes; through Him (that is a process), Amen.

In Philippians 4:19 it says, "My God shall supply every need of yours according to His riches in glory in Christ Jesus." He does not say every spiritual need, but every physical need, every mental need, every material need, every need—spiritual, mental, physical, material is met. Where does God say He will meet it? In Christ. How will He do it? "My God shall supply every need of yours according to His riches in glory." Do you believe it?

Do you really believe that every promise is "Yes" in Christ and through Him will be the fulfillment, the Amen? Do you really believe that every spiritual blessing is yours in Him? Do you really believe that every need of yours can be met and is met in Him gloriously, richly, fully? Do you believe that in Him is all the fulness?

Eternal Life is a Person

I could go on and on. I could talk about life. Eternal life is not a thing; eternal life is a Person. Eternal life is the Lord Jesus who said on more than one occasion: "I am the life; I am the resurrection and the life." He is the life. That is why John the apostle in his first letter says: "And the witness is this that God gave to us eternal life, and this life is in His Son. He that hath the Son hath the life; he that hath not the Son of God hath not the life" (1 John 5:11–12). It is one of the most extraordinary things that the theme you find in conferences and convocations and conventions among Christians all over the world and the subject of so many books that have been written is the Christian life, the Christian life. You hear everywhere, the Christian life. Not once do you find the term Christian life in the Bible. Isn't that extraordinary! Does it mean there is no Christian life? It is not in the Bible. You would get quite upset with me and say, "You mean there is no Christian life?" What the Bible calls eternal life is the Christian life. It is very simple.

And the witness is this that God gave unto us the Christian life, and this Christian life is in His Son. He that hath the Son hath the Christian life, and he that has not the Son of God, no matter how much he has been christened or baptized or registered on some church register, has not the Christian life. Spurgeon once said, "You can be baptized all the way from Land's End in Britain to New England in the United States and all that will happen will be that you will get very wet." The fact of the matter is this: God has given us life, life more abundant, resurrection life, and in that life is exceeding great power, power to overcome every difficulty.

God has placed everything in His Son. And if you are a child of God and saved by the grace of God, He has positioned you in Christ. Through His grace, God has positioned you where all the supply is. Now even more wonderful is that Christ is in you. That means all the supply is actually not far away. It is in you, if you are a child of God.

I do not know whether it sinks in. I know I heard messages like this and they just went over my head. It is a very strange thing that when it came home to me that the Holy Spirit had been given to me I thought to myself: I did not even hardly know there was a Holy Spirit. Yet I had sung hymns about the Holy Spirit. I must have heard messages about the Holy Spirit. It is amazing, isn't it? God has given us everything in Christ, and then by His grace He has placed us in Him and He is in us. But we have to grow in Him. "Christ in you, the hope of glory."

Walk in Him

Then he goes on and says, "As you received Christ Jesus the Lord, so walk in Him." Did you hear that? How did you receive the Lord Jesus? You received Him as a sinner. By the grace of God you received the Holy Spirit, so walk in Him. Don't get big-headed. Don't think you are something when you're not. Walk in the same way you received Him.

What is a walk? Some Christians seem to think that they have to jump. In other words, their whole Christian life is a great series of jerks. Somehow you are blown along by some spiritual, nuclear explosion that blows you up, just like at Cape Kennedy where they go off into space. Somehow that is the way you become spiritual. Rubbish! You may have enormous experiences, but there is no substitute for walking.

What is walking? It is step after step after step. It is a series of steps taken by grace through faith. "By grace have you been saved through faith and that is not of yourself; it is the gift of God." If you see Christ in you, it is not as if you are mature, full-grown, complete. (The old version uses the word perfect, which gives a wrong idea, as if you have no sin at all or any weakness or failing. What it means is you are full-grown.) You may have been saved by the grace of God through faith but you are a baby.

What an excitement it is the first time a baby gets hold of something and stands. There is enormous excitement. Everywhere in the family it is exclaimed: "Little Tommy has stood up!" It is as if it is a kind of miracle, but this is something that has happened a million, million times through the history of mankind. But when it first happens in a family everyone is excited. Phones ring; grandmother and grandfather are told: "Little Tommy has stood up." There is even greater excitement when he takes his first steps.

Isn't it sad when Christians become stationary, immobile? They cannot walk. No matter who you are or how old you are in the Lord, we all have to walk in Him. Did you notice that? "As you received Christ Jesus the Lord, so walk in Him." And as you walk in Him step by step, stage by stage, you grow.

It is a marvelous thing to be a child of God. I often wonder how anyone lives without the Lord Jesus in this world in which we live. Do you ever think that? How does anyone live in this world of ours with all its sorrow and sin, problems, difficulties, without the Lord Jesus? We have to grow up in Him. It is a step by step thing.

Strengthened with Power through the Holy Spirit

In Ephesians 3:16 the apostle is praying and he said, "That He would grant you according to the riches of His glory that ye may be strengthened with power through His Spirit in the inward man."

The only way we can know the Lord Jesus is through His Spirit. How did He dwell in you? It is by the Spirit of God—that you may be strengthened with power through His Spirit in the inward man. That is the first thing.

Here is the second thing: "That Christ may dwell in your hearts through faith." This is the walking in Him. The only way Christ can dwell in your hearts is by the Holy Spirit and through God-given faith. You take step after step sometimes in the face of enormous difficulties, obstacles that seem to demonically laugh at you and mock you, but you believe Jesus is the conqueror. And only when you come through do you look back and say: "I have learned something." Something more is yours of the Lord Jesus through that experience.

Here is the third thing: "That Christ may dwell in your hearts through faith to the end that ye, being rooted and grounded in love, may be strong to apprehend with all the saints what is the breadth and length and height and depth, and to know the love of Christ which passeth knowledge."

I think it is one of the most wonderful things as a believer to know the love of the Messiah, which passes understanding. Height, depth, breadth, length—what a fathomless sea! You will never get beyond the love of God. There is a lover of your soul who will not let you go.

Dear child of God, I find this so amazing—strengthened with power through His Spirit in the inward man, Christ dwelling in our hearts through faith, the breadth, and length, and height and depth of the love of Christ which passes understanding.

Then it says, "Filled unto all the fulness of God." That would be blasphemy if it were not in the Book. How can a little person like me, one little human being be filled unto all the fulness of God? What it means is I am swallowed up by Him. Some Christians have a God so small He is confined, He has boundaries. It is a tremendous thing to be filled unto all the fulness of God. It does not mean that I can contain in my little self all the fulness of God. What it means is I am lost in Him.

I remember years and years ago reading a sermon Campbell Morgan preached. He said, "Why do Christians always think that arriving in the glory is like a ship coming into the harbor. I think of it as a ship setting out to sail." In other words, it is not that everything narrows down and narrows down and narrows down, but the horizon becomes broader and broader and broader, an eternity of exploration, an eternity of experience, an eternity in Christ in glory.

Now I will go through it again. "Strengthened with power through His Spirit in the inward man; Christ dwelling in our hearts through faith, that we might know the breadth and length and height and depth, the love of Christ which passes knowledge, filled unto all the fulness of God. Now unto him that is able to do exceeding, abundantly above all that we ask or think, according to the power that works in us." We are back to the Holy Spirit.

"Strengthened with all power in the inner man through His Spirit . . . according to the power that works in us." This is Christ in you by the Holy Spirit. Do you really believe you have a Lord who is able to do exceeding abundantly above all that you ask or think, or have you limited Him? Is He some kind of idol, a Jesus idol? He can go so far; He can do so much, but you have set Him limits. He cannot do this; He cannot do that. "He is able to do exceeding, abundantly above all that we ask."

Many of us are afraid to ask. I came to the Lord through C. T. Studd and I always remember this little story. He said, "Why ask the Lord for an egg if you can ask for an elephant?" In other words, let your prayers be big. You have not because you ask not. Ask! "Exceeding abundantly above all that we ask or think." Some of us dare not verbalize it. We dare not put it into words. We only think: "If the Lord would only do so and so."

"The power that works in us." Are you limiting the power that works in you? The more of Christ, the more glory; the less of Christ, the less glory. One day everything born of God in you, born of the Lord Jesus in you, begotten of God will be glorified. The more there is of the Lord Jesus in your life the more glory there will be. Some people have got an idea that the kingdom of heaven is a kind of Soviet, a kind of Marxist state where everybody is supposed to be equal. There will be the same amount of glory—no rivalries, no jealousies. Nothing like that. Everyone is exactly the same. It is nonsense! One star differs from another star in glory, it says in 1 Corinthians 15. And if the Lord by His Holy Spirit is able to work in you a greater and greater capacity for the Lord Jesus, there will be more glory. Let me put it this way: there will be more to be glorified. Your capacity for the Lord Jesus has to be enlarged.

"Christ in you, the hope of glory." Unfortunately, today the way we use hope is not the way the Bible uses hope. We use it as a kind of wishful thinking. We hope against hope. It is Christ in you, hoping against hope for glory. That is the way we think. It is a kind of "maybe." I am a child of God. I just hope that I will reach the glory. That is not the way this wonderful word hope is used. This is a certain hope, more certain than the coming of the dawn. We hope for the dawn, that is, we wait expectantly for the dawn. Christ in you is the hope of glory. He is the certain hope of glory (although the word certain hope is not in the original). Is Christ in you? Are you born of God? Has God positioned you in the Lord Jesus? Has the Lord Jesus come into you? That is the certain hope of glory.

What is our problem? Here it is in Colossians 3:2: "Set your mind on the things that are above, not on the things that are upon the earth. For ye died, and your life is hid with Christ in God. When Christ, who is our life, shall be manifested, then shall ye also with him be manifested in glory." Set your mind on Christ.

With Unveiled Face

II Corinthians 3:17–18 says, "Now the Lord is the Spirit: and where the Spirit of the Lord is, there is liberty. But we all, with unveiled face beholding as in a mirror the glory of the Lord, are transformed into the same image from glory to glory, even as from the Lord the Spirit."

It is the Holy Spirit again. It is the Lord Jesus, the glory of the Lord Jesus. It is the light of the knowledge of the glory of God in the face of Jesus the Messiah, but you cannot know that apart from the Holy Spirit. It is the Holy Spirit who reveals Jesus to us, enables us to turn our eyes upon Him. For the saints who are older in the Lord, you may have known the Lord and experienced the Lord for many years but maybe you have a lot of problems, a lot of difficulties. Your eyes have turned away from the Lord. They are on the enemy, they are on the problems, they are on the situation, they are on the difficulties. Turn your eyes upon the Lord Jesus. Only the Holy Spirit can enable you to do that.

"With unveiled face." Do you know what the problem is among so many Christians? They have a veil over their face. "Well," you say, "how could they have a veil over their face?" Unconfessed sin—that is a veil.

Disobedience. You know very well what you are being disobedient on. It could be the smallest thing in your life that the Spirit of God has put His finger upon and you will not listen. That means you have a veiled face.

Worldliness. That is another problem. We get so worldly. We love the things of the world. It veils our face.

Let me tell you a little story that has come back to me recently. Many years ago, more years than I care to remember, at Halford House, at the Lord's Table, a girl came in off the street. She was a waitress at a reasonably well known little restaurant in the town. She had no Christian background. At the Lord's Table we always said, "If you are not the Lord's and cannot commit yourself to the Lord, do not take the bread and the wine." As the bread was being broken and the wine poured into the glasses, she saw the Lord.

She came up to me afterwards and said to me: "While the bread was being broken and the wine was being poured out of that decanter into the glasses I saw the Lord. Instead of the person I saw the Lord, and I have committed myself to Him."

So I said a few things to her about being faithful to the Lord, always obeying the Lord, whatsoever the Lord does, do it; the normal things. She had a great smile on her face and she said, "Thank you." As she went out the door she wheeled around and said, "Oh, there is one thing, one thing I am not going to do."

And I said to her, "What is that?"

She said, "I am not taking this lipstick off."

"But," I said, "nobody has talked about lipstick. Did you hear anyone talk about lipstick or makeup?"

"No," she said, "but I noticed a lot of the ladies are not wearing anything on their faces."

"Well," I said, "that is their business. Maybe they like to be natural."

She said, "I am not taking it off. I have a very pale skin and I do not want to look like a ghost."

I said, "My dear girl, will you make a promise to me?"

"Yes," she said. "What is it?"

I said, "Promise me you will never take that lipstick or that makeup off unless the Lord speaks to you."

"I will," she said. She made the promise and out she went.

It must have been about nine months later I suddenly noticed in one of the meetings, no lipstick. So I went straight up to her afterwards and said, "What about the promise?"

"Oh," she said, "the Lord spoke to me."

Now, I do not see anything wrong in cosmetics or lipstick. I think it is much better to look alive than like a whole lot of corpses just about to drop into their coffins. And if the Lord has spoken to you it does not mean that it is forever and ever. After a few years she actually had her lipstick back. But that one act of obedience brought her into a dimension of spiritual understanding, and from that point she grew. When God speaks to you about giving up television, giving up a sport, giving up novels, giving up this, giving up a friend, giving up a relationship, you may argue and argue and argue. If you do argue and say, "Well, I do not see anything wrong in this; it is legitimate; it is not sinful," a veil comes over your face. You do not behold anymore the glory of the Lord even as in a mirror. So often an act of obedience on so small an issue leads you into a universe of spiritual understanding. Upon small acts of obedience hinge enormous revelation and experience of the Lord Jesus.

"We all with unveiled face beholding as in a mirror the glory of the Lord are changed into the same image as from glory to glory." What does that mean? I can tell you only from my own experience. If I look back on my life I cannot see that it is from glory to glory. I can only tell you it is from tribulation to tribulation. But I have discovered that that is exactly what it means. Every time the

Lord puts you into a difficult situation and you are at your wit's end, He enlarges your capacity for Christ. At the end of that you have more of the Lord Jesus, more of Him. It is a smaller capacity for glory to a greater capacity for glory. This is the work of the Holy Spirit.

So dear child of God, do not give up. Do not give up. The Lord has saved you. There is a beautiful little word in Isaiah that says, "The Lord redeemed Jacob and will be glorified in Israel." Jacob was a twister. There was very little that was glorious about Jacob, but when God met him and touched the seat of his strength and broke him, he became Israel. God redeemed Jacob, but he will be glorified in Israel.

Are you a Jacob? Do not give up. The worst Jacob in the world can see the face of God and live. Then Jacob becomes Israel and Israel is the ground of glory. May the Lord work in you. May He take this little phrase in Colossians 1:27 and apply it to our hearts: "The riches of the glory of this mystery among the Gentiles, which is Christ in you, the certain hope of glory."

Shall we pray?

Beloved Lord, our prayer is that You will touch our hearts. We can hear all these words, hear illustrations, but unless, Lord, by Your Spirit You touch the eyes of our heart and grant to us that Spirit of wisdom and revelation in the knowledge of Yourself, unless You enlighten the eyes of our hearts, it is all to no avail. Therefore, we call upon You. If there is anyone with a veiled face, help them to turn to You in honesty, confess any sin, be done with any compromise, leave any worldliness, obey You in whatever You are asking. We know, Lord, that by Your Spirit You will give new vision, new illumination, new revelation. Hear us, for we ask this in the name of our Lord Jesus, the Messiah. Amen.

3.
The Path to Glory

I Peter 5:10–11

And the God of all grace, who called you unto his eternal glory in Christ, after that ye have suffered a little while, shall himself perfect, establish, strengthen you. To him be the dominion for ever and ever. Amen.

II Corinthians 3:17–18

Now the Lord is the Spirit: and where the Spirit of the Lord is, there is liberty. But we all, with unveiled face beholding as in a mirror the glory of the Lord, are transformed into the same image from glory to glory, even as from the Lord the Spirit.

II Corinthians 4:7–12, 16–18

But we have this treasure in earthen vessels, that the exceeding greatness of the power may be of God, and not from ourselves; we are pressed on every side, yet not straitened; perplexed, yet not unto despair; pursued, yet not forsaken; smitten down, yet not destroyed; always bearing about in the body the dying of Jesus, that the life also of Jesus may be manifested in our body. For we who live are always delivered unto death for Jesus' sake, that the life also of Jesus may be manifested in our mortal flesh. So then death worketh in us, but life in you...Wherefore we faint not; but though our outward man is decaying, yet our inward man is renewed day by day.

For our light affliction, which is for the moment, worketh for us more and more exceedingly an eternal weight of glory; while we look not at the things which are seen, but at the things which are not seen: for the things which are seen are temporal; but the things which are not seen are eternal.

Shall we pray?

Beloved Lord, we are so thankful we are found here in Your presence. We are not asking You to join us; we are coming to join You. You are here as Lord, You are here as Head. We come into Your presence with much thanksgiving and joy in our hearts. And Lord, as we come to the ministry of Your word You have not left us to our own energies, to our own talents or gifts, but You have provided us with an anointing that this time may be sanctified to Yourself, set apart for Your use. Therefore Lord, since You have provided that anointing, we stand into it by faith for the speaking of Your word and for the hearing of Your word. Let the Holy Spirit write these words on our heart. Let something happen within us from the youngest to the eldest that will somehow give us a new sense of direction, a new understanding of Your ways with us. Hear us, oh Lord. We commit ourselves to You with much thanksgiving. And we shall be careful to

give You all the praise and all the glory for answering this our prayer.
We ask it in the name of our Messiah, the Lord Jesus. Amen.

I have had on my heart the phrase you will find in the first letter of Peter 5:10: "Called unto his eternal glory in Christ." Glory is a word greatly misunderstood in Christian circles. They have tried in some of the new versions to give substitute words for it—splendor, magnificence, honor. A whole number of words have been suggested and used, but in fact there is no substitute word for glory. The Holy Spirit has to take this whole truth, this reality, and reveal it to us.

It is the same with the word grace. You cannot really give another word for grace. You have to understand what grace is, and only the Holy Spirit can do that. Without grace there is no glory. Glory is the goal; grace is the way. I call them divine twins— grace and glory.

The Cross

There is a path to glory in Christ, which must be traveled and there is no alternative. In Colossians 3:3–4 it says, "For ye died, and your life is hid with Christ in God. When Christ, who is our life, shall be manifested, then shall ye also with him be manifested in glory."

He died. Your life is hid with Christ in God. This is not just theology. To those whom the Lord has revealed this truth it is absolute reality. "You died and your life is hid with Christ in God. When Christ, who is our life, shall be manifested, then shall you also be manifested with Him in glory."

You cannot go very far on this path to glory and not meet the cross. It is not beautiful. It is stark and bloody and there is no escaping the cross. When Jesus preached the gospel as it is recorded in Mark 8:34-35 for instance, and in other places in the Scriptures, He called the multitude together with His disciples and He said, "If any man follow Me let him deny himself, [give up all rights to himself], take up his cross and follow Me. For whosoever would lose his life for My sake and the gospel's shall find it and whosoever shall save or preserve his life shall lose it."

The word life there is the word "psuche" from which we get psychology, psychologists, and all the rest of it. It is our self-life, our soul-life. He who lays down his self-life for My sake and the gospel's finds his self-life under new management, in a new way, and with a new power. He who preserves his self-life will find it corrupts like cancer before his eyes. It spoils before his eyes.

When you are young, you do not believe this kind of thing. It is only when you get older that you believe it. You have lived long enough to see misery, a people who preserved their self-life in all its forms and tried to satisfy themselves, fulfill themselves, and never trusted Lord. What has happened is very simple. They have lost their self-life. There is no other way to glory than by laying down your life. If you hold on to your rights, you will not come to glory. I am not saying you will lose your salvation. I am saying you will be saved by the skin of your teeth. There will be very little glory.

This gospel we preach today is a pathetic gospel. It is not like the gospel that was preached in the early church nor in every great movement of the Spirit of God in the history of the church. For whenever the gospel was truly preached, there came a command to repent, a command to forsake sin, if necessary to make restitution, to turn to the Lord Jesus and commit your life to Him as Lord and Savior. It was a command.

Today our gospel preaching is basically like a presidential election. We appeal to people. We ask them to make a decision. We bring before them all the wonderful things that will be theirs if they accept the Lord, if they decide for the Lord—heaven not hell, life not death, joy not misery, peace not unrest. Where do you find this? Of course, it is all in the Bible. I am not saying it is not in the Bible, but when the gospel was preached all through church history under the anointing of the Spirit of God, the challenge was: "Lay down your lives. Let go of your self-life. Become a servant of God." That is the meaning of being justified from sin, the meaning of being declared righteous in the sight of God, the meaning of becoming a child of God. You are to become good soldiers of the Lord Jesus Christ, enduring hardships. You are to become warriors in the place of prayer. You are to become worshipers when everything is going wrong, worshipers in spirit and in truth. When you have the gospel preached as it ought to be preached, men and women come under conviction of sin and go through anguish.

In church history, whether it was the Wesleyan (the first great evangelical awakening), or the second great evangelical awakening, or in the Reformation, or under the Puritans, or the Covenantists, or the Quakers, or the Moravians, or the early Calvinists, wherever you look, it is all the same. People would fall down in the meeting place in anguish and agony of mind.

When Jonathan Edwards, who was so short sighted that he had to hold his notes up to his nose with a candle over his head, preached his sermon, "Sinners in the Hand of an Angry God," thousands were saved. They thought they were slipping into hell. They hung on to the pews because they actually thought they were slipping into hell. It was the gospel that was being preached. Then you had strong births of anguish, conviction of sin, a terrible sense of being lost, a sense of being forsaken almost. People came into peace with God. They came into a real conversion. When there were strong births, there were strong Christian lives. When there are weak births, when somehow or other people come to the Lord for what they get and not to follow Him whatever the cost, there are weak Christian lives.

Jesus very simply said, "If any man follow Me, let him give up all right to himself." Are you holding onto the right to yourself? Give up all right to yourself, take up your cross, and follow Him.

I do not know of any better illustration of this little word, "Ye died and your life is hid with Christ in God," than the one I heard years ago. Someone took a little sheet of paper and their Bible and said, "This Bible is Christ; this sheet of paper is you." God lives in the ever present. There is no past with God and there is no future with God. He is I AM. It is as if Jesus died at this moment. God took you and put you in Christ. and when Christ died, you died. And when Christ was buried, you were buried. When Christ was raised from the dead, you were raised from the dead. Wherever I put this Bible, what happens to the note? It is in the Bible. You cannot see the note; the note is in the Bible. Whatever happens to the Bible happens to the note. The history of the Bible is the history of the note because the note is in the Bible.

God took you and put you in Christ thousands of years before you were even born. The ever-present One, the living One, the I Am took you and put you in the Lord Jesus. When the Lord Jesus was crucified, you were crucified. When He died, you died. When He was buried, you were buried. Thank God for that. You were buried—out of sight. Some of us are so much in sight. Then you have been raised with Him to walk in newness of life.

You cannot get to glory without the cross. The cross stands in the path to glory. If you try to avoid it, if you try to soften it, if you try somehow or other to devalue it, you find you are out of the way. You become religious. You are no longer walking in Him. "You died; your life is hid with Christ in God. When Christ who is our life shall be manifested, then shall you also be manifested with Him."

Some people get the idea that this is a kind of dark, hidden, holiness teaching. We are going to have this holiness teaching— so awful. We should all dress in black and look miserable. This is not getting at anyone who is dressed in black, but you should wear clothing as if you are in mourning if you hold onto your self-life. And I say to you younger ones that you will live to remember my words because that self-life of yours has the poison of the serpent in it. It will destroy you. It will destroy your marriage, it will destroy your family, it will destroy your business colleagues, it will, in the end, destroy you. It is only when we let it go, when we lay down our self-life that suddenly we see the poison of the serpent is in it, the sting of the scorpion is there. But when we don't lay it down, we think it is beautiful, we think it is lovely. We think that if we only hold onto it we are safer with it in our hands than in God's hands. Our idea is that God wants to mangle us. He wants to steam roller over us. He wants to give us a bad time. He wants to make us miserable. We have got this idea that anything that has to do with the will of God, of necessity, has to be miserable.

But when you lay down your self-life for His sake and the gospel's, you discover it. It is given back to you under new management, and there is laughter in your soul. There is joy in your soul. There is life such as you never knew before. The poison has gone.

I want to talk about the path to glory and I have to begin there. There is no other way. There is nowhere else we can begin, so you have to face this matter. If you want to come to the glory of God you have to let go of that self-life of yours.

Now you may say to me: "How do I crucify myself?" It is impossible to do that. You can get one hand on the cross, but what about the other hand? You cannot do it. People say, "I am going to try and crucify myself." So you end up with this kind of Eastern idea. If you can do damage to your flesh, if you can sit up on a pole for twenty hours, or starve yourself for months on end, afflict yourself, wear horsehair shirts as they did in the Middle Ages, and things like that, then of course you can do it. No, my friends, you cannot. Don't worry your heads. If you will only give up all right to yourself and take up the cross beam (not the cross) on your shoulders and go to the place of crucifixion, having the sentence of death upon yourself, the Lord will take care of your crucifixion. For you young people, you will find your parents will have crucified you within twenty-four hours. For some of you, your wives will have crucified you within hours or your husbands, and certainly the church. Oh, let the church get their hands on you and they will crucify you with joy while singing a hymn.

Everywhere I go people say to me, especially young people: "How can I live this Christian life?" I always say the same thing: "Don't bother your head about living the Christian life. The secret of living the Christian life is the secret of how to die. Once you die, the life takes care of itself. Once you let go and lay down your self-life, the Spirit of God takes over and suddenly, spontaneously, resurrection life comes, but only when you walk by faith. It is very hard for any normal human being to lay down their self-life, to let go of their self-life, to lose their self-life because they feel that once they have lost it, it will never come back."

Then they say, "I must have made a terrible mistake. The Lord will simply liquidate me. He will annihilate me."

We have this funny feeling about God: "I shall be a monk or maybe a nun. I will live a life of abstinence, a life of affliction." You will live a life of affliction; there is no doubt about it. But with it there will be laughter and joy and fulness, and there will be fulfillment. So we have to start here. It is not how to live the Christian life; it is how to die. And I guarantee that within a few hours at the end of this meeting you will have had your first opportunity to die.

Suffering a Little While

"The God of all grace, who has called you to his eternal glory in Christ, after that ye have suffered a little while, shall himself perfect, establish, strengthen, settle you." Do you hear that? "The God of all grace who called you to His eternal glory in Christ, after that you have suffered a little while ..." The path to glory is suffering a little while. Now God's little while is often a lifetime. I always feel the Lord has enormous humor when He says, "After that ye have suffered a little while."

"We all with unveiled face beholding as in a mirror the glory of the Lord are transformed into the same image as from glory to glory." It does not seem like from glory to glory; it seems more like from tribulation to tribulation, from affliction to affliction, from problem to problem, from being at wits end to another being at wit's end. That is what it seems to be like, and actually that is true because when the Spirit of God speaks "from glory to glory," He is speaking positively.

Actually, the way you go from glory to glory is that capacity is worked in you by problem, by difficulty, by impossible circumstances or situations, and you go from one into yet another. But what the Lord is doing is enlarging your capacity for glory. Every time you come through by faith, through grace, by the God of all grace, there is more of the Lord Jesus in your life. When the Holy Spirit breathed a portion of the word into your heart and you stood on it by faith when everything seemed impossible, and you come out of it to the other end, that word of the Lord has come to dwell in you. It is forever yours. It is no longer just objective Scripture. It is come into you. It is your experience. The word of Christ is dwelling in you in all wisdom and knowledge.

What is the end of suffering for a little while? It is that you may be perfected, that is, full-grown, mature. It does not mean without sin or weaknesses or failings, but you have become mature; you have grown up. Don't you grow up in suffering? Even in normal life, isn't it so? We are children and then all of a sudden someone dies in the family, maybe father or mother, and suddenly we grow up. We have been carried until that moment. Everything has been done for us. Now suddenly we have to grow up. We come through that experience with something we never had before. That is just on the natural scale, those who are unsaved as well as saved. But in the spiritual you are perfected, you are established, that is, you've got foundations. Your feet have touched the bottom. You are on the foundation which is Jesus, the Messiah. You are strengthened. Your confidence in the Lord has been strengthened. You have suffered a little while. In the old King James Version, what we used to call the Authorized Version on the other side of the Atlantic, it has an added word—settled. "Perfected, established, strengthened, settled, after that ye have suffered a little while."

Consider Romans 8:15–17—"For ye received not the spirit of bondage again unto fear; but ye received the spirit of [placing] adoption, [actually the Bar-mitzvah], whereby we cry, Abba, Father. The Spirit himself beareth witness with our spirit, that we are children of God: and if children, then heirs; heirs of God, and joint-heirs with Christ; if so be that we suffer with him, that we may also be glorified with him." So there is an "if—if so be." It is not automatic that we shall come into our reward. "If so be that we suffer with him, that we may be also glorified with him." There is an "if" in this.

How can we possibly go from tribulation to tribulation, from problem to problem, from one set of circumstances that seem impossible to another set of circumstances that seem even more impossible? How can we do it? What value is there in this?

The apostle says, "Our light affliction which is but for a moment." I love this—but for a moment! I think it is for a lifetime sometimes, but he says, "but for a moment." Why? It is because he is weighing it against eternity. If we weigh our affliction by our little three score years and ten, it is a lifetime. If we measure it by what we gain in eternity it is a pinprick. It is light affliction but for a moment, transient, so temporal, so fast. Our light affliction which is but for a moment worketh for us an exceeding and eternal weight of glory. Can you believe that? Light affliction-weight of glory–but for a moment-eternal working for us.

Do you realize the word here is to employ? God employs the light affliction to work for us an exceeding and eternal weight of glory. If we look at things which are seen, it is stupid to be a Christian. If we look at the things which are seen, why not go out and enjoy ourselves for tomorrow we die? But if we look at the things which are not seen, then to go out and enjoy ourselves because we think life is so transient, that is stupidity. "An exceeding and eternal weight of glory; light affliction but for a moment—eternal glory, exceeding great and eternal glory."

Eternal Treasure

Here is the process. This is the path to glory. "We have this treasure in earthen vessels." Only God could put eternal treasure in clay pots. Some of us are a little more "potty" than others. We are just clay pots. Some of us are a little cracked. Normally, when people have treasure, such as diamonds, they do not put them in clay pots.

I remember going to the diamond center in Ramat Gan in Tel Aviv. The man, who was one of the really big diamond dealers of the world, was a survivor of Auschwitz. He knew that my family, fifty-eight members of it, my father, my grandmother, and fifty-six other members died in Auschwitz. And he said, "Would you like to see the diamond exchange?" I have always been interested in diamonds, so I said, "Yes, I would love to go see the diamond exchange." I have never forgotten this. He took a pouch from a safe and turned it upside down on a tray, and he said, "There is about four hundred and sixty thousand dollars here." Treasure. He put that treasure in an enormous safe, and I fully understand because the Mafia in Israel is fifty per cent Arab and fifty percent Jew and they work very well together.

If you have jewels, diamonds, sapphires, rubies, unbelievable wealth in treasure, you would not put it in a clay pot, would you? Only God can take eternal treasure which is Christ Himself and put it in us—Christ in you the hope of glory, the certain hope of glory. That is treasure; that is real treasure. That is eternal treasure. He takes the Lord Jesus and causes Him to indwell us by the Holy Spirit—in little, old clay pots like us. Only God could do it.

And he explains why: "That the exceeding greatness may be from God and not from ourselves." It is not because we are anything, because we are clever, because we are zealous, because we are devoted, because we are knowledgeable, because we are good and decent [that God has saved us], but we are saved by the grace of God. And God, if I may so speak of Him reverently, has taken the risk of putting the treasure in such as you and me. Have you ever realized what a price God puts on you? Do you realize how much the Lord really loves you, that He could have placed in you eternal treasure?

The Way the Treasure is Produced

But this treasure has to be worked. This is a testimony: "Pressed on every side; perplexed, pursued, smitten down." I have never heard any believer get up and give his testimony or her testimony and say, "I am pressed on every side; I am perplexed; I am pursued; I am smitten down." We would say, "Send him to a deliverance ministry. He needs deliverance. Something is wrong with him. After all we send people to Bible college, theological seminary, so they won't be perplexed. Who wants leaders that are perplexed? We do not want someone perplexed. We want them to know what to do and how to do it and then tell us." But here is the great apostle saying, "I am perplexed, but not unto despair. I am pressed on every side, hard pressed in some of the modern versions, but not straitened; in other words, not in a straitjacket. I am persecuted, pursued, but I am not forsaken."

I thought the Christian life was a life of joy. I thought the Christian life was being carried by the power of God into glory. There is nothing like the joy of knowing God when you have laid down your life.

You see, God never causes you to suffer for a little while unless you are prepared to suffer. If you want to be one of these Christians who hangs on to your own self-life, gives it toys to play with, tries to satisfy everything, tries to advance its self-fulfillment, God leaves you to it. You are saved, you will be in the kingdom, but He leaves you to it. Your tears will come later. But for those who shed tears now in impossible situations, they will have no tears when the glory of God is manifested.

"Pressed on every side, yet not straitened. Perplexed yet not unto despair; pursued but not forsaken; smitten down ..." (Phillips put it this way: "knocked down but not knocked out.") "Always bearing about in the body the dying of Jesus that the life also of Jesus may be manifested in our mortal body." Now think: "always bearing about in the body the dying of Jesus." So what does this mean? All this experience is something to do with bearing about in the body the dying of Jesus, being delivered up to death. You say, "How does that happen?" Your boss will deliver you up to death. Your employees will deliver you up to death. Your husband will deliver you up to death. Your wife will deliver you up to death. Your children will deliver you up to death. Your parents will deliver you up to death. And the church will certainly deliver you up to death.

"Always being delivered up to death that the life also of Jesus may be manifested in our body." So on one side you have the negative—bearing about in the body the dying of Jesus. On the other side you have the positive—that the life also of Jesus may be manifested in our mortal bodies. This paradox is the path to glory.

"So then death worketh in us but life in you." Only those of us who minister the word of God under the anointing of God know at times how it is death in us. But then we hear of blessing. People always ask me, "Wasn't that wonderful?" I do not know whether it is wonderful or not. All I know is that I have to give a word, and I find that I have to stand by faith.

I always remember the story that either Whitefield or Wesley, one of those two extraordinary servants of God, wrote in his journal. He stood before those thousands and thousands of miners, and in the journal, whoever it was said, "I felt so dead. I felt like dry bones, and I was tempted after preaching for a few minutes to close the meeting, but I went on in faith. And then suddenly I saw an extraordinary sight. I saw all the faces of those people streaked like zebras—black-white, black-white, black-white." Suddenly he understood they were weeping under conviction of sin.

Those miners were considered by society in general to be subhuman, animals. Nobody had any time for them, and when they came up in their thousands to listen to Whitefield and Wesley, the employers got very angry. They actually asked members of Parliament to raise the question in the British Parliament because they said, "They should not be standing and listening to someone preaching when they are paid to work." Of course what they were paid to work was a pittance.

"So then death works in us but life in you." That is the path to glory.

Now I want to take you to Philippians 3:10 where the apostle says, "That I may know Him and the power of his resurrection and the fellowship of his sufferings."

"That I may know Him." In the Greek there is a little prefix: "That I may fully know Him and the power of His resurrection." Doesn't every child of God want to know the power of His resurrection?

"And the fellowship of his sufferings." There is no way to come to the eternal glory in Christ apart from the fellowship of Christ's sufferings.

There is something quite mysterious to me in this word in Colossians 1:24: "Now I rejoice in my sufferings for your sake, and fill up on my part that which is lacking of the afflictions of Christ in my flesh for his body's sake, which is the church whereon I was made a minister."

Oh, for more ministers like this, for more servants of God like this! I rejoice in the afflictions that I am suffering because it is for the body's sake, which is the church. It is not just a matter of preaching; it is not just a question of a platform ministry; it is much more than that.

What does he mean, "That which is lacking of the afflictions of Christ"? I can only understand it this way. You and I cannot in any way enter the sufferings of Christ, which were for our salvation. That is unique to Him. But the Lord has left a portion of His suffering to be filled up by the members of His body. That is the only way I can understand it. This is the fellowship of His sufferings. It is wonderful to know the power of His resurrection—but the fellowship of His suffering? These two things go hand in hand.

Or again, look at what Peter says, "Beloved, think it not strange concerning the fiery trial among you, which cometh upon you to prove you, as though a strange thing happened unto you: but insomuch as ye are partakers of Christ's sufferings, rejoice; that at the revelation of His glory also ye may rejoice with exceeding joy" (1 Peter 4:12–13).

"The elders therefore among you I exhort, who am a fellow-elder, and a witness of the sufferings of Christ, who am also a partaker of the glory that shall be revealed." 1 Peter 5:1

You cannot be a partaker of the glory of the Lord Jesus that will be revealed unless you are prepared to be a partaker of His sufferings. Is this morbid? People think, "Couldn't we hear about the power of the Holy Spirit? Couldn't we hear about the fulness of the Holy Spirit? Couldn't we hear about the exceeding greatness of His power?" Yes, you can, and I would be only too glad to speak about it, but now I am speaking about the path to glory. And there is no way to come to the glory, eternal glory in Christ, apart from being a partaker of His suffering. You have got to settle it. There is no alternative to this.

The Thorn in the Flesh

Paul speaks about the thorn in his flesh. You will find it in II Corinthians 12:9: "And God hath said unto me, My grace is sufficient for you: for My power is made perfect in weakness."

We don't know what the thorn was. Some people get very upset if you say it was a physical illness. They say, "Of course not! The apostle Paul didn't have any physical illness." So what was it? Who was it? Maybe it was a person. Maybe it was John Mark. I can well understand that. I wonder. No, it was some thing. In Conybeare's Translation, which is so to the point, this thorn in the flesh is called: "The agony of impalement."

This thing was so colossal. It was not some little thorn. We know that when you get a thorn the whole foot or hand can swell up. It can be a really unpleasant experience. The apostle Paul is not talking about that kind of thing. What the apostle Paul is talking about is something so colossal that he thought it was the end of his ministry. Three times he besought the Lord:

"Remove this thing; it is from Satan." And the Lord said to him: "My grace is sufficient."

Now of course, when we are terribly spiritual, we feel that if the Lord said, "My grace is sufficient," that's it. But a bit later the apostle went back to the Lord and said, "You have got to remove this thing. I know You said Your grace is sufficient but You have got to remove it. I cannot fulfill this ministry if this remains." And the Lord said, "No Paul, My grace is sufficient. For the weaker you are the more powerful I am in you." Treasure in earthen vessels. Treasure in a clay pot that the exceeding greatness may be from God and not from Paul. That is the path to glory.

The Proving of Your Faith

Let me take you another step. In 1 Peter 1:7 the apostle says, "That the proof of your faith, being more precious than gold that perisheth though it is proved by fire, may be found unto praise and glory and honor at the revelation of Jesus Christ."

I do not like the old version's word trial. "The trial of your faith." In my estimation it still has a negative feeling. (In the old days, maybe test was a good word for this Greek word.) When someone is on trial you feel that everything is in question, but that is not what the Spirit of God is saying. He is saying, "I am testing you because there is something in you that can be tested. I am not trying you to see if there is something in you." The Lord never brings a trial on some Christians because it would kill them. It would finish them off. The Lord never does it. But where there is real God-given faith, then the Lord proves it.

Do you remember how Peter said, "Lord, don't You worry; You are not going to the cross, not while I am around." And the Lord said to him: "Peter, before the cock crows you will have denied Me three times." Then He said this: "Simon, Simon," (using his Hebrew name) "Satan has obtained you by request that he may sift you as wheat; but I have prayed for you that your faith fail not. When you are turned around, remember."

Peter had a whole self-manufactured Christianity. He had walked with the Lord for three years. He had heard the Lord. He said marvelous things by revelation: "Thou art the Messiah, the Son of the living God." The Lord Jesus said, "My Father in heaven revealed that to you." Of course, most preachers would say that Peter was one of these who always puts his foot in it. But actually all the rest did too. It was Peter who always spoke.

Isn't it true of all of us? We all say, "Oh, so and so," but in actual fact it says, "And so said all the others." But it was Peter who got the blame. He was a natural leader, but that quality of personality in him, his Christianity as such was self-made, self-manufactured. In one single moment it was blown to pieces by a spiritual, nuclear explosion when a little, tiny, serving girl danced up to him and said, "You are one of His disciples." And he said, "Me? Never! I do not know the Man." Three times he said it, and the cock crowed. All it took was one look from Jesus on His way to execution; one look and Peter wept. It was not like Judas who committed suicide; he wept his way back to the Lord. That meant his God given faith, deeper than all his self-manufactured Christianity, stood the test. It was the proving of his faith more precious than gold that perishes. It was to be found in praise and glory and honor at the revelation of Jesus Christ.

The Lord will never put you through anything unless there is something that He knows is of Himself. Satan has desired you that he may sift you as wheat. Isn't it amazing! Satan gets the chaff and God gets the wheat. You may lose all your self-manufactured Christianity. Every servant of God has to come to it sooner or later, but God gets the wheat and Satan gets the chaff.

C. T. Studd once said, "Satan is God's most used servant." No wonder he got into so much trouble with Christians. It is so true. God uses Satan. Didn't He use him with Job? Satan got all the chaff; God got the wheat. So it is with your treasure.

Material for the City

The treasure of Christ is material for glory. It is the most remarkable thing that the city of God at the end of the Bible sums up everything—the bride and the city. It is a most extraordinary bringing together of two very different ideas. Do you not think it is remarkable that there are only three materials out of which that bride, that city is produced—gold, precious stones, pearl? All three of these materials speak of the Lord Jesus—the gold of His nature and life; the precious stone of His excellencies, of His character; the pearl of His suffering.

When the Lord Jesus spoke to the Laodicean church, He said, "I counsel you, I advise you to buy of Me gold refined in the fire that you may become rich." In another place, in the Corinthian letter, the apostle speaks about wood, hay, stubble. That doesn't sound very pleasant, does it?

I remember years ago on a number of occasions in Manila going to the Coconut Palace. Imelda Marcos' Coconut Palace was the VIP guest house for the government. Everything in that amazing place is made from coconut, from the things you walk on, to the lampshades, to the walls, to the lamps. I could not believe it. I had no idea that you could use coconut so much. I had always only thought of eating what is inside of the coconut.

Wood, hay, stubble can be so beautiful. Many Christians have coconut palaces they have built out of wood, hay, and stubble. It looks marvelous. The façade is tremendous. There is Christian life, there is knowledge of the Bible, but it is wood, hay, stubble.

When you come to the city, to the bride, it is only gold, precious stones, and pearl. Gold in its natural state has to be sought, mined, properly refined. Precious stone is found in the dark places of the earth. It is produced by pressure and heat. You cannot just see it. Pearl—in the heart of every real pearl is a bit of worthless grit, a little bit of debris that fell into the softest part of the clam.

In Genesis 2 you find a river. There is a tree of life in the midst of the garden and somewhere where the tree of life is, there is a river of life. This river goes out into four great rivers. Then we are told that if you follow the river you will find gold, and the gold of that land is good, it says. You will discover bdellium, which is the Greek name. In Hebrew it is bedolach. And you will find onyx stone. It may not mean much to you but first of all let me say all these things could be easily overlooked. You could ignore them; you could sail down the river and not even know there is gold in the riverbed or in the riverbanks. You could traverse over the ground and not even know that under it is onyx stone. You remember the high priest had twelve great stones on his breastplate. But when he took those twelve stones, representing the whole people of Israel on his shoulders, it was onyx stone on each of his shoulders. There were six names on one shoulder and six names on the other shoulder, as if onyx stone symbolizes all the precious stones.

But the most remarkable of all is the bdellium. Bdellium is a little aromatic plant. When you break it, a white substance comes out that hardens and looks like a pearl. The rabbis believe and I believe also that there was one little mistake here because bedolach means this plant but badal means pearl. It is almost deliberate by the Spirit of God to throw you off scent.

At the end of the Bible you have gold, precious stone, and pearl. And at the beginning of the Bible you have gold, precious stone, and pearl, but it is hidden. You could easily walk past it. You could easily think there was nothing there, nothing.

Do you know that in the tragedy in your life there is a pearl in the making? Or are you overlooking it? Do you know that the situations you are in, the problems you are in, the obstacles you are facing, there is precious stone there, hidden, unmined, undiscovered? It is there. Do you know that in the relationship that you find impossible, which you think is destroying you, whether it is with children, or parents, or husbands, or wives, or a great aunt, or grandparents, there is treasure?

You and I can just go through like a river cruise and never know that there is gold in the land, never know that there is precious stone, never know that there is pearl. We, by the Spirit of God, through faith, have to mine the gold. We have to find the stone. When we come to the end of the Bible, the pearls have become the gates, the gold has become the street and everything in the city, and the precious stone is the foundation. The gold is so refined that it is transparent as crystal. The precious stone has been cut, polished, faceted, set. The pearls, huge pearls, such as you and I have never seen, have become the gates.

When Amy Carmichael was a young missionary, she used to be known for the way that she had always run back and forth between the different houses of the children, her hair streaming behind her, her sari streaming behind her. I knew people who had worked with her for years. Then came the opportunity to open a new work in a town nearby in India and they went. When they got there, the man who should have come with the key was two hours late. When he came, the tropical dusk had fallen. He unlocked the gate, swung it open, and they waited for Amy Carmichael to go first. She fell into a huge ditch that had been dug by coolies in the wrong place. She broke her wrists, her hip, her ankle. She was carried in the jeep in great pain over rough roads for an hour or two until they got her to the hospital.

Amy Carmichael had no idea that one whole phase of her life was finished and her real ministry had begun. She wrote a little book that may be known to some of you—Rose From Brier. In it she apologized and said, "You know, I think I have been six months with this problem, only six months, and I feel guilty trying to help others who are suffering." She had no idea that there would be thirty plus years more on her back. Yet out of that came something incredible. She wrote a poem:

> ... *But from thy brier shall blow*
> *A rose for others. If it were not so*
> *I would have told thee. Come, then, say to Me,*
> *My Lord, my Love, I am content with Thee.*

I always commend Amy Carmichael's books to those who are suffering inexplicable suffering. There are few such books that can touch the heart. It is deep calling to deep.

I think of Fanny Crosby when she was young. She had some irritation in her eye and they called the doctor. He came, but he came with the wrong liquid. He put acid into her eyes and it burnt her cornea. She never saw again. Out of Fanny Crosby came the hymns that a whole number of generations sang.

I think of Horatio Spafford who was called by God to Jerusalem. He was a successful lawyer who found the Lord Jesus through D.L. Moody. When they got to New York, his wife, his four girls, and the governess got on the ship. He went back to Chicago to settle some things and planned to join them later. On a perfectly calm night during a full moon the ship had a head-on collision with another ship. His four daughters and the governess were drowned. His wife, who was eight months pregnant, had gone down three times and was brought up by the mast of the ship that came up between her knees and carried her to the surface. She managed to get to England where Horatio Spafford was going to join her. The boy that was born to them died a few months later.

When Horatio Spafford was on the ship going to England, the captain came to him and said, "I think we are about as near as we can be to where you lost your daughters." He sat down and wrote the hymn: "When peace like a river attendeth my way, when sorrows like sea billows roll."

I think of George Whitefield who was born with a cast in his eye. One eye looked one way, the other eye looked the other way. They called him Captain Two-eyes. Every time he preached on sin at least two people in the congregation got convicted.

Beloved friends, there is gold in the earth and we do not know it. It is the gold of Christ's life and nature. He is advising you to discover it. Buy it with experience. That is the only cost—experience. There is precious stone, material for the glory.

Faults Made the Focal Points of Beauty

My great-uncle was one of the great jade experts and lived his whole life in Beijing. He was a lover of antiques, which unfortunately I have inherited. I think it is in the blood stream. When I was first saved, an old missionary came to us and she stayed with Auntie Dagmar. She was one of "the trio" in Northwest China. And I have never forgotten her talking about jade in Auntie Dagmar's drawing room. Later she gave a series of messages on it and it was put into a booklet: The Parable of Jade. She entranced and fascinated me as a boy of fourteen when she told how the master jadesmith would get the apprentice to take down from a shelf a great rock of jade wrapped in silk. They would undo it while he was drinking green tea. The master jadesmith would look at it and then it would be wrapped up again and put up. Generally, it was because there was a flaw in the jade. There was a beautiful white jade with one dark brown spot. There was a beautiful pale green jade with a kind of orange color just in one spot. What was the jadesmith doing? He was trying to think what he could do with that jade to create a masterpiece and somehow take the fault and make it the focal point of the masterpiece. If you have ever been to some of the great galleries in Washington or other places you would have seen a pure white lotus with a bee on its petal. The bee, which is so beautiful, so finely crafted, is the focal point of the beauty of the piece. The fault has become something of eternal beauty. You see a green piece and there is a dragonfly or sometimes a little frog.

That is what God does with our lives. We have made terrible mistakes; we have made a fault. We feel we cannot get over it but God is the master jade smith. He takes that life and He works on it and in the end He makes the mistake the focal point of beauty. He did it with David. When King David fell into sin with Bathsheba and had her husband murdered, they lost a child. God took David, broke him, remade him, and both Solomon and Nathan, the two in the Messianic line, were born of Bathsheba. Only God can take even the sinful disobedience and mistakes in our lives, when confessed, and weave them into something of eternal beauty. This is the pathway to glory. This treasure is in earthen vessels, that the exceeding greatness may be from God and not from ourselves.

Are you ready to walk this way? Are you ready to let God do His work in you? You young people, when you are so young, full of life, full of energy, full of fun, it is hard for you to think you must lose your self-life. That self-life of yours will destroy you unless you are prepared in an act of faith to let go of it for Him. You will never regret it. Never! Never! Not through time, nor through eternity, will you ever regret letting go of your self-life and committing yourself to the Lordship of Jesus.

Shall we pray?

Oh beloved Lord, do reach our hearts this night. Convict us in this path to glory. Convince us by Your Holy Spirit. There are some of us fighting with problems and obstacles, relationships that are impossible, tragedies that have come into our lives. Lord, will

You apply this word as comfort and encouragement to our hearts. In the name of Jesus, our Messiah. Amen.

4.
The House of Glory

1 Peter 5:10–11

And the God of all grace, who called you unto his eternal glory in Christ, after that ye have suffered a little while, shall himself perfect, establish, strengthen you. To him be the dominion for ever and ever. Amen.

Deuteronomy 12:5–7, 11

But unto the place which the Lord your God shall choose out of all your tribes, to put his name there, even unto his habitation shall ye seek, and thither thou shalt come; and thither ye shall bring your burnt-offerings, and your sacrifices, and your tithes, and the heave-offering of your hand, and your vows, and your freewill-offerings, and the firstlings of your herd and of your flock: and there ye shall eat before the Lord your God, and ye shall rejoice in all that ye put your hand unto, ye and your households, wherein the Lord thy God hath blessed thee ...
Then it shall come to pass that to the place which the Lord your

God shall choose, to cause his name to dwell there, thither shall ye bring all that I command you: your burnt-offerings, and your sacrifices, your tithes, and the heave-offering of your hand, and all your choice vows which ye vow unto the Lord.

Isaiah 11:10
And it shall come to pass in that day, that the root of Jesse, that standeth for an ensign of the peoples, unto him shall the nations [Gentiles] seek; and his resting-place shall be glorious.

Isaiah 60:7b
And I will glorify the house of my glory.

(This word is a different word in Hebrew. The other word is the normal word for glory, but this word has the idea of beauty as well. It is not just glory but it is beauteous glory. Some versions have it:

"I will beautify my house with beauty.")

Isaiah 60:13
The glory of Lebanon shall come unto thee, the fir-tree, the pine, and the box-tree together, to beautify the place of my sanctuary; and I will make the place of my feet glorious.

Psalm 132:8, 13–14
Arise, O Lord, into thy resting-place; Thou, and the ark of thy strength...For the Lord hath chosen Zion; He hath desired it for his habitation. This is my resting-place for ever: Here will I dwell; for I have desired it.

Haggai 2:6–9
For thus saith the Lord of hosts: Yet once, it is a little while, and I will shake the heavens, and the earth, and the sea, and the dry land; and I will shake all nations; and the desire of all

nations shall come; and I will fill this house with glory, saith the Lord of hosts. The silver is mine, and the gold is mine, saith the Lord of hosts. The latter glory of this house shall be greater than the former, saith the Lord of hosts; and in this place will I give peace, saith the Lord of hosts.

Ephesians 2:20–21

Being built upon the foundation of the apostles and prophets, Christ Jesus himself being the chief corner stone; in whom the whole building, fitly framed together, groweth into a holy temple in the Lord; in whom ye also are builded together for a habitation of God in the Spirit.

1 Peter 2:4–6

Unto whom coming, a living stone, rejected indeed of men, but with God elect, precious, ye also, as living stones, are built up a spiritual house, to be a holy priesthood, to offer up spiritual sacrifices, acceptable to God through Jesus Christ. Because it is contained in scripture, Behold, I lay in Zion a chief corner stone, elect, precious: And he that believeth on him shall not be put to shame.

Shall we pray?

Beloved Lord, as we have remembered You and all Your great love for us, we come very simply now to You and ask that You will take the ministry of Your word and use it to bring illumination and understanding to all our hearts. Only Your Holy Spirit can do that. And Lord, we pray for that spirit of wisdom and revelation in the knowledge of Yourself to be granted to us. Even if we have seen these truths, we need to see them more deeply, more clearly than ever before. We need to see their application to our lives, to our homes, to our families, to our assemblies. Lord, only You can do this. We thank You that You have provided us with an anointing and into that anointing of grace and power we stand by faith for both the speaking of Your word and the hearing of Your word. Dear Lord, meet with us. Touch our hearts, Lord. Bring us into a new way with Yourself, a new understanding of Your purpose in our day and generation. And we shall give You all the praise and all the glory, for we ask this in the name of our Messiah, the Lord Jesus. Amen.

Glory is a very misunderstood, devalued word in Christian circles. We use it in a very light-hearted way: "Glory, oh it is glory," without really understanding what we are saying. There is no substitute word for glory. Magnificence, splendor, honor—these words do not really convey the reality and truth that is in this word glory. Only the Holy Spirit can reveal this to us. But once the God of glory appears to a child of God that life is spoiled for anything less than the glory of God.

We see in the God of glory the city of God, the Messiah of God, the kingdom of God, the throne of God, the people of God, the redeemed. Once the God of glory appears to us, we see in the God of glory the Messiah and we see in the God of glory the city of God, the bride. We see in the God of glory the treasure that God puts into our lives through all the difficulties and afflictions and tribulations that we pass through. It is a tremendous thing. It is no wonder to me that it is the God of all grace who calls us to this eternal glory. We are not worthy of it. We do not deserve it. We are sinners who fell short of the glory of God. But He is the God of all grace and He has taken hold of worthless debris, flotsam and jetsam that you and I are in this world and brought us into a new way with Himself.

It goes right back to Abraham. God took hold of him, and ever since He has been taking hold of people and bringing them into His purpose. Isn't it an amazing thing that you and I have joined people like Abraham and Isaac and Jacob and Joseph and Moses and Joshua and Samuel and David, and on and on. It is amazing to me the company of the elect of God, called by the Lord, chosen by the Lord, saved by the Lord, who have been called into His eternal glory in Christ.

It is a wonderful thing to know the Lord, and these two words grace and glory go together. They are divine twins. You cannot part them. You will never come to glory without the grace of God. Grace and glory belong together.

The Home of God

Now I want to take this little phrase in Haggai: "I will fill this house with my glory." It is an amazing thing! If only it was the Lord and me, but you have got the intimation that it is more than me, more than you that is involved in this thing.

Colossians 1:27: "Christ in you." One of the best things about the old version is the English because there you have thee and thou and you and ye. When you was used it is always plural, so you had a distinction. Now everyone uses you, you, you, so you do not know whether it is just an individual or whether it is plural. But it says, "Christ in you, and you, and you." It is not just Christ in me. The glory of God is far too great for one person.

The eternal glory of our Lord Jesus is far bigger than me. I cannot reveal and manifest that glory. It cannot be just manifested in me adequately. It needs all the saints through the whole of time, all the redeemed to express the glory of God in Christ, the eternal glory of God in Christ.

You have an intimation there that this matter of Christ in us, the certain hope of glory, has a relationship to others. It would be much easier if it was just me. For one thing you can be deluded when it is just you. You can coast along and do your own thing, but it is the saints who are the problem. Once we have other people journeying on the same path and we have to be related to them, disciplined by them, and somehow stay with them, that is the biggest problem we have.

You have the same thing in Hebrews 2:10 when it says about the Lord Jesus that He is bringing many sons unto glory. It is not enough to bring you as a son. Whether you are a lady or a man you are a son of God, you are a child of God. It is not just a question of bringing you, personally, to glory; He is bringing many sons to glory. Therefore, in every generation there has to be relationship—relationship to other believers who are journeying on this same path to glory.

That brings me to this whole matter of the house of God. It is amazing to me the typology that you have in the Old Testament. It is not going too far to say that this matter of the tabernacle or the temple is a focal point of God's eternal purpose in the old covenant. You will find it everywhere. Once your eyes are open you will discover that this question of God's resting place, God's habitation, God's home (which is a better word), God's dwelling place, is everywhere.

You have the two books of Samuel, the two books of Kings, then you go over the whole thing again in the two books of Chronicles. Why? Why does the Lord go over the whole thing again? These four books, Samuel and Kings, are all to do with the throne and the kingdom, but Chronicles says, "At the heart of the kingdom is the home of God." We see everything in Chronicles from the viewpoint of the house of God, the home of God, the resting place of God.

The Place Where His Name Dwells

Have you ever asked yourself why we have this extraordinary phrase throughout the Old Testament, the old covenant? "The place where I will cause My name to dwell"; or "The place I will put My name." Don't you think that is an extraordinary phrase? Most Christians are so used to their Bible they never ask these questions. It just sort of goes in one ear and out the other: "Of course, it is the place where He puts His name to dwell. It is the place where His name dwells." But surely a name does not dwell in a place. What does it mean?

For one thing, names in the Bible have far greater meaning than the way we use names today. We often choose names for our children that are pretty, that have a nice feeling, but not in the word of God. In the word of God people's names were often prophetic of their whole destiny and their whole character. A name represented the person. God's name, the name of God represents His heart, His mind, His character, His being, His purpose, His kingdom, His throne, His redemption. "I will cause My name to dwell there." In other words, the Lord wants something that represents Him, that expresses Him, that expresses His heart and His mind, a place where He can be absolutely Himself, where He can rest. It is not a place to visit, or bless, or use, but a place where He is at home.

In the old covenant you have this whole amazing thing. It seems as if so much of the Old Testament is all to do with the building of the house of God or the rebuilding of the house of God or the completion of the house of God. It is everywhere: in Zechariah, in Haggai, in Malachi, in Isaiah, the great evangelical prophet. Everywhere you turn you will find this extraordinary thing.

God chose Jerusalem, and it was there that His habitation, His dwelling place, His resting place was built. Now all of that has a tremendous amount for us.

There was a prophet whose name was Zechariah. He was very much involved in the completion of the second temple. You remember he had a vision one day in which he saw two olive trees and a seven-branched, golden lampstand. He understood immediately that this was the menorah, the lampstand in the temple. On either side was an olive tree and branches came out of the olive tree and liquid gold. (Your version says golden oil but there is no oil in the Hebrew.) It is gold that comes out of the olive tree into the lampstand and becomes fuel for the light.

Zechariah, like so many of us, was more interested in himself and his ministry than in the heart of the thing, and he said to the angel, "Who are these?"

And the angel said, "Not my might, nor by power, but by my Spirit, saith the Lord of hosts. Who art thou, O great mountain? Before Zerrubabel you shall become a plain, and he shall bring forth the top stone with shoutings of Grace, grace, unto it" (Zechariah 4:6).

Then it speaks about the plumbline. In other words, it is all to do with the building. His hands began the work, His hands shall complete the work. Suddenly we understand this whole vision is not just to do with the house of God as a theology; it is to do with a building program. It is to do with a divine, eternal, building program. So the lampstand is not just representative of the church; it is representative of something more—the practical application of the church. So many of our assemblies are all caught up with the truth. That is all we ever see. We are not bothered about evangelism, we are not bothered about outreach, we are not bothered about souls dying around us, we are not bothered about getting out to the world. All we are concerned about is the theology of the church. That is not the church!

The church is the place where saints are built into Christ. They are related one to another. They grow up into the Head, the Lord Jesus. That is the church. The church is the place where man meets God and God meets man. It is a place where the nations come, the unsaved, the Gentiles, as it used to be in the old covenant, and in the old version, heathen. They come into this house of the Lord for it shall be called a house of prayer for all nations. This is something that hits us; it impacts us. We begin to realize this is not just a truth upon which we are focused, upon which we are centered. This is a building program, and God takes the seven-branched, golden lampstand as the symbol of this building program. There have to be spirit filled men and women. Without those Holy Spirit filled men and women, there can be no functioning church. It is a theology. But where the Holy Spirit pours the life of Christ into a few believers, a building begins to take place, a relationship begins to be produced by the Holy Spirit, and there is light.

I hope I am not being too severe on us, but we are basically second generation, and that is the greatest danger in the history of the church. That is where we turn living power into systematized theology.

"I will cause My name to dwell there." Do you believe that you can have the building of the church without compassion for a dying world? Do you mean to tell me that you can have a church which does not care at all about the nations, about the nation in which it is found? That is a contradiction in terms.

In the New Testament, the new covenant, the bride shares the name of her husband, Jesus. Take the home of God; it is a home that shares the name of Jesus. Take the city of God; it is the name of the Lord that is in that city. Take the body of the Lord Jesus; it does not have a different name to its head. It shares the name. "I will cause My name to dwell there."

When we come to the last book of the Bible, we see John the apostle turning around because he hears a trumpet sound behind him and a voice speaking. He sees seven golden lampstands. They, of course, represent seven churches in seven different localities—one church in seven localities. It is a lampstand. Jesus says to Ephesus, of all places, which was one of the better churches: "If you do not repent I will come and remove your lampstand out of its place."

Does that mean that the routine ceases? Of course not! The Bible studies will go on, the prayer meetings will go on, the breaking of bread will go on, all the routine of the church will go on, but the lampstand has gone. What does that mean? It means the building has stopped. The thing has become a memorial; it has become a gravestone. It has died. The building work of the Holy Spirit has stopped.

This is the testimony of Jesus. That lampstand all of gold represents the testimony of Jesus. We hold that testimony, just as the lampstand holds the seven lamps. What is the point of a lampstand if there is no light? We hold that seven-fold lamp and it is light: Light to the believers, light to the afflicted, light to the poor, light to the world.

God's Resting Place

What a beautiful thing the Spirit of God said to Isaiah the prophet: "His resting place shall be glorious." In the Hebrew it is simpler. It just says, "His resting place shall be glory." When they set up the tabernacle, the moment everything was completed and everything was in place, the glory of the Lord filled it. They could not enter because of it. When they set up the temple and everything was in place, when the ark of the covenant had been brought in and all the vessels of the temple were in their place, the glory of the Lord filled it and the priests and Levites could not stand up to minister. It was a wonderful picture—"His resting place shall be glory."

It is everywhere. What a wonderful word that is in Psalm 132: "Arise into Your resting place, Thou and the ark of Thy strength." That is the presence of the Lord. Then the Psalmist says, "For the Lord has chosen Zion. He has desired it for His home. This is my resting place forever. Here will I dwell."

There is no temple in the city. The Lord God and the Lamb are the temple. And there is no need of the light of sun or moon, for the Lord God and the Lamb are the light of it. It is the glory of God that lightens it. This is so tremendous!

I was a Baptist and a very zealous one. I thought there was nothing like the Baptists, but when the day came that I saw what the church was, in a single moment of time I was not a Baptist. It is not that I am against the Baptists. I am everything actually. I believe in the Anglicans, the Episcopalians because of their parish church. I believe that is local, absolutely right. One church divided by where you live. I don't have any problem with that. I am a Presbyterian because I believe in elders, and I believe in the conferring of elders with elders. I am a Baptist because I believe there is no other kind of baptism than baptism of a believer by immersion. That is the Jewish form of baptism anyway. They tried to tell us that it wasn't. Now we know from all the latest archeological discoveries that it was very common. I am a Quaker because I do not believe that things are institutional. I am an open brother because I believe that the priesthood of all believers must be given place. I am a Pentecostal because I believe in gifts and even a Charismatic. I am the lot. But when I saw what the church was, I saw that it included every born again believer. I belong to them and they belong to me. In that moment I ceased to be a Baptist and became a Christian.

When you look at this matter of a home of God in the Spirit, in John 2:18 it says, "The Jews therefore answered and said unto him, What sign showest thou unto us, seeing that thou doest these things? Jesus answered and said unto them, Destroy this temple, and in three days I will raise it up. The Jews therefore said,

'Forty and six years was this temple in building, and wilt thou raise it up in three days?' But he spake of the temple of his body."

John 1:14 says, "The Word became flesh and tabernacled among us." Jesus is the fulfillment of the typology of both the tabernacle and the temple. When the Lord Jesus was raised from the dead it was, as it were, another kind of temple that was now raised. Then we begin to understand something.

In Ephesians 2 it speaks of a home of God in the Spirit. So you and I are meant to be God's home by and in the Holy Spirit. Quench the Spirit, grieve the Spirit, and the whole thing is just a theory. We who have been saved by the grace of God are meant to be a home of God in the Spirit.

A Holy Temple in the Lord

This is the second thing: "A holy temple in the Lord." Have you ever heard of such a thing? The Lord Jesus said, "Destroy this body and in three days I will raise it up." "A holy temple in the Lord." Are you in Christ? I am in Christ. That means you and I have a relationship. We may not like each other. We may be temperamentally different, racially different, culturally different. There could be a thousand and one things that could be a middle wall of partition between me and you and you and me, but it has all been done away by the finished work of the Lord Jesus. And the most wonderful thing is that as I am in Christ, so you are in Christ, and if Christ is in me, so He is in you. Now we have an incredible relationship with one another.

I find by the grace of God that I am in Christ, but I do not have a personal Christ. I think it is a terrible term—a personal

Christ as if you have your own tailor-made Christ, one who is accommodating to you, one who is adjusted to you. There is only one Lord Jesus. He is the Savior and Lord of us all. I am in Him and you are in Him. He is in you and He is in me. Now we have a two-fold relationship. We are in the same One and the same One is in us. Now we have a spiritually organic relationship. I belong to you; you belong to me. Why do I belong to you? Why do you belong to me? It is because I belong to the Lord Jesus and you belong to the Lord Jesus. You have been born of the Spirit of God; I have been born of the Spirit of God. Now we have a relationship. The whole building fitly framed together grows into a holy temple in the Lord. Isn't this amazing?

"A home of God in whom..." (In whom? In Christ.) "... builded together as a home of God in the Spirit."

The Process of Building

"Groweth into a holy temple in the Lord." "Fitly framed together, groweth into, builded together into a home of God in the Spirit." It is a process. That is where all our problems come. That is the focal point of our problems. If only somehow or other this whole thing was a fait d'accompli, something accomplished, something that is a fact, already done. It is completed. No, no, no; this is something you grow into. This is something you are builded together into.

Now we have the problems. If I could only choose the people that I could be builded together with into God's home, it would be so much nicer. But it is not like that. God takes people so different from us and He puts us together. We have to stay together, and that is the biggest problem in church life. If I could only say to you: "Good-bye. The Lord is calling me to another fellowship just down the road. The point is that I have found it a little too hot with you. It is a little bit too difficult. I would prefer to go to this one."

But of course I won't stay there. Normally, it is out of the frying pan into the fire because your problem goes with you. You are the problem, and when you go off somewhere, you take the problem with you. I hear it all over the place: "The testimony of Jesus is gone. The headship of Jesus is gone." It is very easy to say that. So we are going to go with the testimony of Jesus, are we? We are going to go with the headship of Jesus? I do not find any such thing in the Book. If there are believers living in your locality that are found on the foundation of the Lord Jesus, you have to stay there. There is no fire escape. It is like being in a pressure cooker; you cannot get out. You can only let off steam now and again. You are being cooked together into a wonderful meal.

Dear brothers and sisters, how deceitful we all are! "I do not find the Lord here" and we are off.

It is a very interesting thing to me that when the Lord spoke to the seven churches in Revelation 2 and 3, He never once said: "Now you who are faithful, leave." Even where there was Nicolaitanism, which meant a hierarchy. A hierarchy had developed in the leadership and the Lord said, "I hate this thing," but He never said, "Leave." He said, "Overcome."

Even in one there was a Jezebel, some woman, apparently a sister, teaching deep things of Satan. (Can you believe it?) The Lord never said, "Leave. You who are faithful, leave." He said, "Overcome."

Even with the Laodicean Church, which was so lukewarm the Lord said, "I am sick of you. I will vomit you out," He never said, "Leave." He said, "Overcome." In other words, this building together of believers is the place where all the problems are centered, and it is our relationship to one another that determines whether we are overcoming. We don't become partakers of other's sins, but we wash their feet. We love them. We care for them. We do not become embittered.

There is a story about Charles Haddon Spurgeon that is very good. He was a great preacher who was always called the prince of preachers because of his silver tongue. About half way into his ministry (He was already at Metropolitan Tabernacle in London), he began to get a letter every Monday morning. The letter was very courteous. It was addressed to him: Dear Mr. Spurgeon. It pointed out his grammatical mistakes in the sermon, his diction mistakes in the sermon, and the mistakes in the content of the message. Of course everyone spoke of Spurgeon as being absolutely superlative and I think probably it got into Spurgeon's mind that perhaps he was.

The great Charles Haddon Spurgeon began to have nightmares because he could not find out who it was. It was obviously someone in the congregation. It came by hand by a courier every Monday, and it robbed him of all his confidence. Can you believe that? You would have thought he could have shaken it off. No, no; it robbed him. And in the end he decided he must get behind the scenes (I'm putting it in my own words) and nail this brother or sister in the name of the Lord. And he began to sort of indulge in spiritual warfare and try to nail this thing down. Then one day the Lord said to him: "Do you want me to remove your treasure?"

And Charles Haddon Spurgeon said, "What do you mean, my treasure? This is not treasure; this is demonic." (I am putting it in my own words.) And then the Lord said to him: "This is how I am producing treasure in you." From then onward, Spurgeon received that letter every Monday morning to the end of his life. And as far as I know, he never knew who it was that sent it.

You know that difficult person you have to live with? Did you know that God is using him or her to produce treasure in you? You know those difficult people in the office? Did you know that God is using that unsaved man, that unsaved woman to produce treasure in you? Did you know that God is using them to make you face the reality of yourself? It is only in this kind of relationship we discover who we really are.

I remember a man, who was a very big man in Christian circles, sending me a letter on one occasion. He said at the end of this long letter: "You know, I am the most humble man in the world." We all knew this brother as the most proud man, but he had no idea. He had come up against another big leader and this leader he said was arrogant and proud. Maybe that explains some of your situations.

I remember another lady, who was Irish (That is a very good thing.). She always used to say to us, "You can tell me anything because I can keep a confidence." But we all knew that if you told Auntie, the whole town would know within one hour, especially if you added, "I am telling you this in confidence." It is amazing, isn't it? Some people are incredibly longwinded. If you tell them they are longwinded they get very angry and upset.

We do not know ourselves. How do we get to know ourselves? It is by relationship. It is not in some high mountain retreat where we are alone with the Lord, and somehow or other in this wonderful place of sunrises and sunsets and twittering birds we suddenly see ourselves. It does not come that way because most of us do not want to see ourselves. We have an idea of ourselves that is quite false. It is unreal. And the façade has to be destroyed by relationship with very difficult people. That is no easy matter. We would rather be a loner: "Me and the Lord. We will go places—the Lord and I. I am on the pathway to glory, just me and my Lord."

It does not work because the Lord sets the solitary, the loner in families, and there we suddenly discover that we have brothers and sisters we have not actually chosen. The Lord has chosen them. That is why so few are Calvinists. They prefer to be Armenians in this matter. They like to think that it is just an accident. It is no accident. Your wife is not an accident. Your husband is not an accident. Your children are not an accident. Your parents are not an accident. The boss at work is not an accident. Your employees are not an accident. And if there is one place where there is relationship which can be very painful, it is in the house of the Lord. What a wonderful thing it is when brothers stay together, but no brothers in leadership can ever stay together without cost. Someone has to lay down his life.

The Cornerstone

In the apostle Peter's first letter he says, "Unto whom coming a living stone [that is the Lord Jesus], elect, precious, ye also as living stones are built up a spiritual house to be a holy priesthood to offer up spiritual sacrifices to God" (1 Peter 2:4–5a).

This living stone, the Lord Jesus, is the cornerstone. A cornerstone is not the house. Why has the Lord Jesus got this title, the cornerstone? In the Old Testament you will find prophecies about the cornerstone again and again. Is it a stone that we put into museums? Is it a work of art that we put in magnificent homes? No! What is a cornerstone? It is to do with a building program. A cornerstone is tremendously important, significant, but it denotes a building program.

Living Stones

The second thing is that a cornerstone and one other stone are not a home. Oh, you say, "I want to get my relationship right with the Lord Jesus. That is the thing that matters, my relationship with the Lord Jesus." A cornerstone and one stone are not a home. You have to have all the living stones finding their relationship to the cornerstone for there to be a house. You can have a great, beautiful pile of stones. If you are German or Dutch they will be perfectly put together. If you are English they will probably be a pile. Certainly, if you are a Californian, it is a pile. But a pile of stones does not make a house, not even when they are tidily stacked. The stones have to find their relationship one to another in relation to the cornerstone; in other words, in relation to the Lord Jesus. Now does this mean something to you?

I remember so well years ago when my home in Jerusalem was renovated. In the 1947-48 War of Independence they had stored all the ammunition up in my loft. Some clever Arab sniper had managed to fire something which blew the whole roof off and the back of the house as well, so they had to renovate it.

In those days the stones all came by donkeys. All those rough rocks came in panniers on either side of the chain of donkeys and they were dumped out in front of the main door of the house. This old stonemason who could not speak a word of English would come with a boy, and they would pick up the stones and take them inside. I have never forgotten how he took those stones up one by one. To this day I don't understand it but I remember the problem I had over it because he would take up a stone, look at it, examine it, and then throw it away. Others he would put in another pile. And I went to look at what he was throwing away and thought to myself: I know what he is up to. He is going to take those back to his own home. (I am not Jewish for nothing.) That man seems such a nice man, a sweet man, but he is a crook. So I went and looked at the stones. They were beautiful. Jerusalem stone is very beautiful. It ranges from gray to yellow right through to a greenish color and to orange and red. I sort of looked at him and he obviously realized what I was thinking but he could not really explain himself. He could only speak Arabic.

In the end, the engineer, the supervisor of the whole thing came to me and said, "I understand you have a problem with these stones."

And I said, "Yes."

He said, "All these stones have flaws. If he were to spend a week on cutting them, chipping them, chiseling them, at the last moment they may split. He knows." Stones that the builders rejected.

He spent weeks on these stones. To this day I think back to that old man. I can see him in my mind's eye now, chink, chink, chink—hour after hour—chink, chink, chink, chipping away.

It is the old handwork. One of the town architects who was one of my neighbors came to me and said, "Oh, I am so glad that you are doing this the old way. Your neighbor, who is one of the wealthiest men in the world, has sawn it all and it is dead. The stone is no longer living; it is dead. It will never show color. The way you are doing it, all through the day and through the seasons, you will have different color." And it is true. In my neighbor's house, it does not matter whether it rains, whether it is mist, or what it is, the stones are always the same color, dull yellow.

The stones that this old man did breathed life. When it rains they go deep, orange red. So beautiful! Living stones. Living stones require handwork. It takes time.

You folks over here and in Europe too I must say, all believe in instant things—instant coffee, even instant tea now, instant cream, instant cakes, instant sponges, instant this, instant that, and we all want instant holiness and instant building together. There is no such thing! The Lord has to work. It takes time; it is handwork—chink, chink, chink. You think you are getting nowhere. It takes time.

"To whom coming a living stone, ye also as living stones are built up a spiritual house to be a holy priesthood to offer up to God spiritual sacrifices." This building work, this lampstand, this testimony of Jesus denotes work, a building work. I am always jealous of you over this side because so many of your homes are wood and they are built so quickly and beautifully put together. God does not use wood; He uses stone. It is a much longer process. But if any of you have had anything done in your home, you will surely know that there is always a mess when builders are at work.

The Church on Earth

Why is it we are always looking for the perfect church? I do not understand this idea. Everybody is looking for the perfect church. I think it was D. L. Moody who once said to a man who said he was looking for the perfect church: "When you join it, it won't be." But we have this idea that we are looking for the perfect pattern, the perfect church, but the perfect church is the city. That is the end product. The church in expression on earth is always imperfect. That is the hallmark of the church on earth. It is imperfect. It is a mess. It is a builder's yard, bits and pieces all over the place. It does not look nice. It is not tidy. It is a building work that is going on. People say, "Oh, I am looking for something perfect." But you will become perfect by being in the messy building work. That is how you will be perfected.

Let me put it another way. Everyone thinks the churches in the New Testament were so perfect. Perfect! What kind of glasses are you using? Take Corinth. They got drunk at the Lord's Table. How they managed to do that on grape juice I do not know, but they got drunk at the Lord's Table. They were gluttonous, greedy at the Lord's Table. I can just hear decent twenty-first century believers saying, "I am leaving. I am not staying with this lot—gluttony, drunkenness. I am not going to be within a hundred miles of this assembly." There was a boy sleeping with his mother. Can you believe it? The church was divided into four sections, three named after great spiritual leaders and one exclusive: "We are of Christ."

Take a good church, Ephesus; there was Nicolaitanism; they left their first love.

Take another church, Thyatira, and you find there Jezebel teaching the deep things of Satan. Can you believe it? "Out! I am out."

The early New Testament church was not perfect. There was a couple who stood up and gave their testimony. One dropped dead and when the other partner came in, she dropped dead. Can you imagine the next church meeting! Some people may have said: "Peter, you are being a bit severe, causing Brother Ananias and Saphira's death like that." No, my friends, the early church was not perfect; it was a mess. And God was doing something in the mess because it was a builder's yard. All the bits and pieces were all around but God was doing something in the lives of those people, perfecting them for glory, building them up into a spiritual house to be a holy priesthood to offer up sacrifices to God.

What is the challenge in all of this? It is very simple. You cannot come to the glory of God, the eternal glory in Christ, alone. It is with your other brothers and sisters that you come. It is through them that the Lord will do such a work in you and through you a work in them. When the Lord has found His resting place, built it, completed it, then His glory fills it. This is God's home, the place He dwells forever. It is hard to believe, isn't it, when we think of ourselves, that we should be the dwelling place of the Lord forever? We do not really know what the Lord will do in eternity to come. All we know is that He has a purpose. That purpose was arrested by sin and by falling short of His glory. There will come a day when the house is complete, the bride is perfected, the city of God will arrive, and with it the glory of God. Then the Lord will say to us: "Now we will get on with the job. What was in Our mind at the beginning in creating mankind We will now get on with the job." Then that glory of God in the people of God will spill out into the whole natural creation and into the whole universe. How marvelous!

Dear child of God, don't give up. Don't throw in the glove. Don't let the enemy defeat you. We are, by His grace, in the train of Christ's triumph. Stay there and by the God of all grace you will reach His eternal glory in Christ.

Shall we pray?

Dear Lord, we know that it takes a committal on our part really to be built together, to have a relationship with one another in You. Lord, this world is filled with division amongst your people, disarray amongst your people, factionalism, and so much else. Oh Lord, have mercy upon us. Will You challenge our hearts? Since we are candidates for glory, since by Your grace You have chosen us to be those who will share in the eternal glory of Christ, Lord challenge us by Your Spirit. Bring in our hearts a committal to Yourself and to Yourself in one another, that however poor our assemblies represented here may be, we will stay together and move together until You have done the work of building in us. Lord, help us. We ask it in the name of our Lord Jesus. Amen.

Other books by Lance Lambert can be found on lancelambert.org

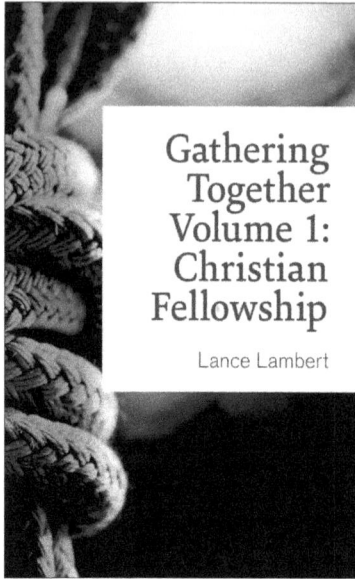

Gathering Together Volume1

What is the church? What is the basis for meeting together as the church? What is true fellowship? What is the priesthood of all believers? What is the difference between unity and uniformity in the church? In this book, the first volume of Gathering Together, Lance Lambert answers these questions and many more. In doing this, he emphasizes the absolute headship of Christ and the oneness of the body of Christ.

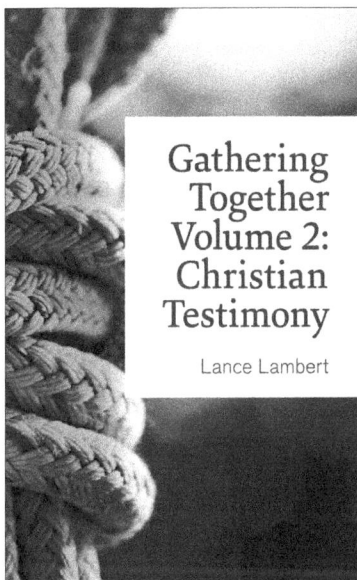

Gathering
Together
Volume 2:
Christian
Testimony

Lance Lambert

Gathering Together Volume 2

Do you want to see the church in practical expression on earth in our day? Do you want to see the glory of the latter house exceed that of the former? What is the secret, the key to the source of the life of God in which everything lies inherent? The house of God is going to be built; it must be built. The top stone will be brought forth one day with shouts of "Grace, grace to it." Let us seek the Lord that we may see that day!

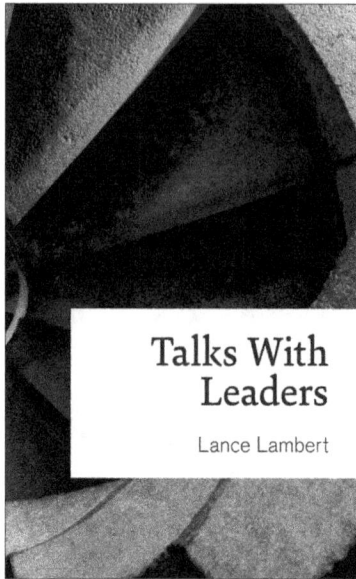

Talks With Leaders

"O Timothy, guard that which is committed unto thee ..." ~ I Timothy 6:20 Has God given you something? Has God deposited something in you? Is there something of Himself which He has given to you to contribute to the people of God? Guard it. Guard that vision which He has given you. Guard that understanding that He has so mercifully granted to you. Guard that experience which He has given that it does not evaporate or drain away or become a cause of pride. Guard that which the Lord has given to you by the Holy Spirit. In these heart-to-heart talks with leaders Lance Lambert covers such topics as the character of God's servants, the way to serve, the importance of anointing, and hearing God's voice. Let us consider together how to remain faithful with what has been entrusted to us.

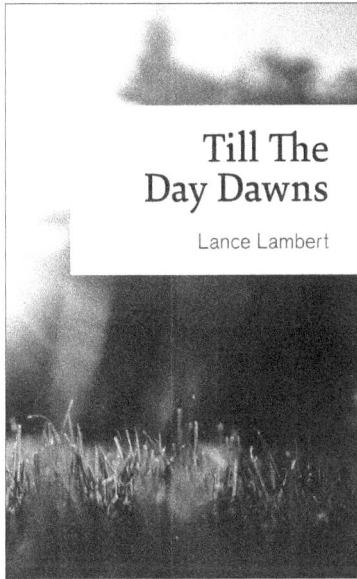

Till The
Day Dawns

Lance Lambert

Till the Day Dawns

And we have the word of prophecy made more sure; whereunto ye do well that ye take heed, as unto a lamp shining in a dark place, until the day dawn, and the day-star arise in your hearts. ~ ii Peter 1:9

The word of prophecy was not given that we might merely be comforted but that we would be prepared and made ready. Let us look into the word of God together, searching out the prophecies, that the Day-Star arise in our hearts until the Day dawns.

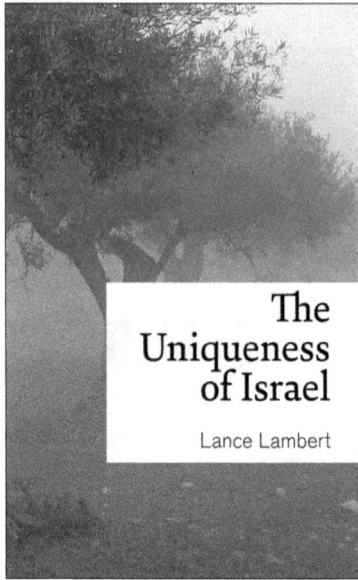

The Uniqueness of Israel

Lance Lambert

The Uniqueness of Israel

Woven into the fabric of Jewish existence there is an undeniable uniqueness. Israel¿s terrain, her history and chief city, all owe their uniqueness to the fact that God¿s appointed Saviour for the world was born a Jew. His destiny and theirs are forever intertwined.

There is bitter controversy over the subject of Israel, but time itself will establish the truth about this nation¿s place in God¿s plan. For Lance Lambert, the Lord Jesus is the key that unlocks Jewish history He is the key not only to their fall, but also to their restoration. For in spite of the fact that they rejected Him, He has not rejected them.